Praise for *Toas*

"Nothing makes a special event as memorable as a heartfelt, personal toast that conveys both wit and sincerity. Enter June Cotner and Nancy Tupper Ling's new book *Toasts: The Perfect Words to Celebrate Every Occasion*, filled with creative ideas, inspirations, and advice on how to create that special remembrance. It is a must on every bookshelf, at every stage of your life."

—Emma Roberts,
author of *Sassy Sips & Nibbles* and owner of Capers Catering

"Life should be celebrated and *Toasts*, the newest offering from June Cotner and Nancy Tupper Ling, not only reminds you of the importance of making the most of every moment, but also gives you the words to do it. Filled with toasts from the famous and not-so-famous, this book offers elegant, eloquent, witty, and true toasts for every occasion. Whether you're tongue-tied before a group and need a little help finding the right words or you are looking to inspire and honor, this book will give you just the right words and sentiment for any occasion."

—Polly Campbell,
author of *Imperfect Spirituality*

"A heartfelt toast can strengthen the bonds of friends, family, and colleagues in good times and bad. This elegant and inspiring book provides tons of creative ideas as well as basic toasting etiquette for those of us who want to make sure we're doing it right. May your toasts be always at the ready!"

—Tina Gilbertson,
author of *Constructive Wallowing:*
How to Beat Bad Feelings by Letting Yourself Have Them

"Toasting is a powerful and exciting pastime that we look forward to at every event as well as cherish in our memory. It makes people appreciate the greatest successes, as well as those little accomplishments along the way. *Toasts: The Perfect Words to Celebrate Every Occasion* not only improves our own speaking skills, it makes us smile when we think back to the toasts we have experienced in our lives."

—David Mezzapelle,
bestselling author of the Contagious Optimism book series

TOASTS

TOASTS

THE PERFECT WORDS TO CELEBRATE EVERY OCCASION

by June Cotner
& Nancy Tupper Ling

Published in the United States by Viva Editions, an imprint of Cleis Press, Inc., 2246 Sixth Street, Berkeley, California 94710.

Printed in the United States.
Cover design: Scott Idleman/Blink
Cover photograph: iStockphoto
Text design: Frank Wiedemann

First Edition.
10 9 8 7 6 5 4 3 2 1

Trade paper ISBN: 978-1-936740-85-7
E-book ISBN: 978-1-936740-99-4

Library of Congress Cataloging-in-Publication Data

Toasts! : the perfect words to celebrate every occasion / [compiled] by June Cotner and Nancy Tupper Ling. -- First edition.
     pages cm
 Includes index.
 ISBN 978-1-936740-85-7 (alk. paper)
 1. Toasts. I. Cotner, June, 1950- compiler. II. Ling, Nancy Tupper, compiler.
 PN6341.T6332 2014
 808.5'12--dc23
                    2013041971

Dedication

From June Cotner:

For my grandchildren
Shay and Weston

From Nancy Tupper Ling:

For my parents
Soli Deo Gloria

Contents

Letter to Readers

A well-chosen toast can make simple moments special, and special moments memorable. Whether it's celebrating a wedding, a job promotion, a birthday, or a new direction in life, toasting is a tradition that remains a part of honoring important occasions. Delivering a heartwarming toast has the power to inspire, uplift, and move everyone present. What better way to celebrate the key moments in the lives of our loved ones than with just the right words?

When it comes to making a toast, knowing what to say and how to say it is a talent that takes practice. *Toasts: The Perfect Words to Celebrate Every Occasion* is the place to find fresh, original toasts in addition to traditional favorites. The confidence and inspiration to make the perfect toast can be found within this diverse and imaginative collection, and you can learn the best way to present your selections in "A Guide to Toasting," which begins on page xvii.

The selections in *Toasts* are inspiring, reflective, uplifting, and sometimes humorous. Beyond standard categories such as weddings or anniversaries, we have included useful toasting categories such as adventures, business events, housewarming, and class reunions, as well as an assortment of toasts for each of the major holidays. These thematic sections are helpful for those in search of a toast for specific events or occasions.

I have been working on this anthology for almost a decade, and I'm delighted that it is finally being published! I am thrilled to be sharing coauthorship of *Toasts* with Nancy Tupper Ling, who is a poet, children's author, and librarian. Nancy won the 2005 *Writer's Digest* Grand Prize for her poem "White Birch." Chosen from over 18,000 entries, hers was the first poem to win over all other categories, including screenplays, poetry, fiction, nonfiction, short stories, children's stories, and young adult fiction. In 2002, Nancy founded the Fine Line Poets (www.fine-linepoets.com), and has served as poetry judge and library liaison for the Massachusetts State Poetry Society.

Toasts contains a rich spectrum of writers, ranging from favorites such as Robert Browning, George Burns, Emily Dickinson, Ralph Waldo Emerson, Robert Frost, Groucho Marx, Carl Sandburg, Mark Twain, and William Wordsworth, to new and original content from contributors like Michael S. Glaser, Arlene Gay Levine, Charles Ghigna, and Barbara Younger.

The toasts in this book are intended to offer words of inspiration and celebration for all of the important milestones in life, and to underscore our recognition of friends and family in those simple moments we want to remember forever. Here's to you and to finding the perfect toast!

Cheers from June and Nancy!
June Cotner (www.junecotner.com)
Nancy Tupper Ling (www.nancytupperling.com)

A special note: for any selection that appears without an attribution, we have determined through extensive research that the piece is "author unknown."

A Guide to Toasting

When proposing a toast, your presentation can make an event memorable, which is a gift for the recipient that will be treasured forever. A well-crafted toast can be delivered by anyone, for any occasion. All it takes is sincerity, planning, and a little bit of personalization. Here are some key elements that can make your toast successful.

KEY ELEMENTS

Sincerity. When you're looking through *Toasts* to find a passage that speaks to you and to the person you're toasting, take your time. Make sure that your toast comes from the heart and touches both the recipient and the other guests at the event.

   Personalization. There are many events in life that call for a toast;

one of the great benefits of *Toasts* is that it offers selections for every life event, big and small. It's important to tailor a toast to the recipient; find something that fits *them*.

Creativity. The passages in every chapter of *Toasts* can be adapted to any situation or individual, whether it's for a wedding, Mother's Day, celebrating an award, or a family reunion.

Respect. Remember that a toast is supposed to honor an event in someone's life. The selections in *Toasts* are not "roasts," but true toasts, quotes, and blessings. We have included humorous toasts, spiritual toasts, simple toasts, short and sweet toasts, and a few lengthier blessings—so you can find a variety of toasts for any occasion.

Propriety. The loved ones gathered at any milestone in a person's life may come from varied backgrounds and age groups. All of the toasts in this book are appropriate for every audience.

PRESENTING THE TOAST

Generally speaking, it is considered polite to stand when offering a toast. Make sure that you've practiced your words a few times, so you're ready when the time comes. At large gatherings, introduce yourself and give your relationship to the guest of honor for those who don't know you. When toasting, it is only necessary to stand and ask for attention, but if this is not successful, you may lightly ping your glass with a spoon. As you make your toast, hold your glass in your right hand, arm out, and slightly upraised.

Once you've given your toast, it is customary to ask the guests to raise their glasses and drink to the recipients of the toast. When clinking glasses, there's no need to stretch across the table; lightly tap the glasses of the people near you, and raise your glass slightly to those far away. A nod and a smile is the best way to share the toast.

One great quality of a good toastmaster is making those around you feel comfortable. Whether you're presenting a funny toast or a heartfelt and serious toast, being calm and collected will put those around you at ease, and make your toast that much more memorable and meaningful. If you are nervous about public speaking, however, it is a good idea to bring a small note card for reference. This backup/guidance is not considered rude. Rather, it is appropriate should you feel jittery about memorizing your toast. The mark of the successful toastmaster is simple: be yourself, give your toast, and have a good time!

A FEW NOTES ON ETIQUETTE

When you are the recipient of a toast, there's no need to sip with everyone else; you are the one being honored! A simple acknowledgment is all that is necessary.

Toasting, but not hosting—it is generally considered polite to thank the host of an event before you begin your tribute to the honoree.

Clear and audible speaking—as we mentioned earlier, practice makes perfect. If you've had the opportunity to practice your toast ahead of time, you will be able to speak more calmly and clearly; everyone appreciates understanding the toast!

Eyes are the window to the soul—make eye contact when toasting!

Let other people know you mean what you say, and want to include them in the moment. Share your words with the room.

Go out strong—end on a positive note, and make people smile. Let everyone know your toast is over by saying "Cheers!" or "To so-and-so!"

The perfect toast is simply the heartfelt expression of joy and celebration of an event, individual, or group of people. *Toasts* will help you find the words you need and the confidence to get up there and speak them proudly. Remember to breathe, smile, and give your toast from the heart.

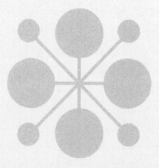

Thanks

As coauthors, Nancy and I are deeply grateful to our agents Anne Marie O'Farrell and Denise Marcil at Marcil-O'Farrell Literary. Anne Marie and Denise spent many hours helping us shape our book into something that would be fresh and appealing to a wide range of audiences, specific toasting occasions, and celebrations.

In addition to reading submissions from many of the 900-plus writers and poets who contribute to my anthologies on a regular basis, we read thousands of possible toasts from writers who found us via Facebook, LinkedIn, Twitter, and various online writing groups.

We are thrilled to be working with Brenda Knight and her fine staff at Viva Editions. At the time our agents approached her about our *Toasts* book proposal, Brenda had a "toasts" book on her radar already, having come to the conclusion independently that a contemporary toasts book with fresh content and a few standard favorites was needed in the marketplace.

Nancy and I had so many wonderful toasts to consider that we decided to undergo a "test market" critique process where potential users of the book would have the opportunity to rate and comment on possible selections. We are deeply grateful to Linnea Pearson, Madeleine Pearson, and Brian Samek for their ratings and comments as "typical" users of a toasts book. In addition, the following poets spent many hours helping us decide on the final content for the book: Sally Clark, who has been published in *Say a Little Prayer: A Journal*, eight of my other anthologies, and whose work is featured in many books, magazines, and on greeting cards; Mary Maude Daniels, writer and photographer, who has been published in *Gratitude Prayers* and eight of my other books; Arlene Gay Levine, author of *39 Ways to Open Your Heart* and *Movie Life*, and contributor to 25 of my collections; Barb Mayer, photographer, writer, and contributor to *Garden Blessings*; Jean Tupper, journalist and author of *Woman in Rainlight*; Donna Wahlert, contributor to 14 of my books, and author of *The First Pressing: Poetry of the Everyday* and *Well into the Third Act*; and Barbara Younger, author of *Purple Mountain Majesties,* creator of the blog, "Friend for the Ride," and contributor to ten of my anthologies. You can find more information about these poets from their websites listed in Permissions and Acknowledgments.

Nancy and I are so thankful for our families and friends who offer encouragement for our writing projects and inspire us daily by the lives they live. The impetus behind *Toasts* was to honor family and friends— and we hope we have accomplished that.

And, most of all, this book would not exist without the hundreds of writers who submitted to *Toasts*. We so appreciate the gifts of creativity you have offered throughout this book!

ADVENTURES

Always be on the lookout for the presence of wonder.
—E. B. WHITE

Life is between the trapeze bars.

I decided a long time ago to keep
checking the door in case
opportunity was knocking.
Are you opportunity?

—LINDA ROBERTSON

I intend to do everything that frightens me.
—GILDA RADNER

Your wings already exist, all you have to do is fly.

May you climb mountains
and swim rivers
and more than anything
may you fly.
—SEAN THOMAS DOUGHERTY

From the joy of discovery
to the thrill of new faces,
your dreams will transport you
to magical places.
—BARB MAYER

May all of your campsites be warm and inviting,
and all your adventures be grand and exciting.
—BEATRICE O'BRIEN

Raise a glass to fighting dragons,
try to catch the wind.
May you always find adventure,
just around the bend.
—LOUISE I. WEBSTER

A BLESSING FOR A HIKE

May our legs be steady.
May our hearts be ready.
May this trail be our friend,
from beginning to end!
—BARBARA YOUNGER

Listen,
around you the world is whispering;
it speaks to your heart.
Look,
the world is showing you the extraordinary
in the mix of everyday life.
Be there.
Be dazzled...
—ZORAIDA RIVERA MORALES

To adventures—
when you keep an open mind,
they can be found where you least expect them.
—BARB MAYER

As you venture forth,
carry in your spirit,
our love and very best wishes.
Here's to your adventures!
  —BARBARA YOUNGER

ANNIVERSARIES

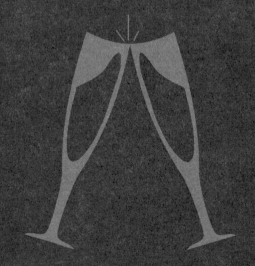

> When I think back on our years of marriage, it is not necessarily the happiest and romantic times that bring the most warmth to my heart. Rather, I like to remember the time our washer broke and we had no money to buy groceries, but we still held hands and laughed.
>
> —KIRSTEN CASEY

ANNIVERSARY OPUS

I love you more than yesterday, less than tomorrow.
I love you for what you are, but I love you
yet more for what you are going to be.
I love you not so much for your realities
as for your ideals.
I pray for your desires that they may be great,
rather than for your satisfactions,
which may be so hazardously little.
You are going forward toward something great.
I am on the way with you,
and therefore I love you.

Here's to you both,
a beautiful pair,
on the birthday of
your love affair.

Here's a toast to marriage—
the greatest educational establishment in the world!

Don't waste your time
on one perfect rose
or box of chocolates—
just warm up her toes.
—WENDY L. SCHMIDT

Let the purpose of all marriages
and friendships alike
be the deepening of the spirit
and the enrichment of the soul.

I celebrate this day with you, my dear;
Here's to another this time next year!

—CARL "PAPA" PALMER

YOU ARE MY STAR

No need to wish upon a star,
you are, you are, my only star;
and should we live another score,
I could not love you any more.

—CHARLES GHIGNA

A TOAST TO MARRIAGE

Blessed be
the best memories
shared with My Love—
a toast to
now and then.
We are
Forever.

—PAULA TIMPSON

The secret to our success is that on the day we were married I let my wife know who was the boss. I looked her right in the eye and said, "You're the boss."

Life is like a roller coaster.
On this ride I want to be buckled in next to you.
No matter what curves may be, we lean together—
you and me.

    —CHARLENE HASHA

Here's to *years* of happiness,
and *months* of sunny skies,
to *weeks* of reaching mountain peaks,
and *days* of caring eyes,
to *hours* of hope and tenderness,
and *minutes* of delight.
On *second* thought, we wish you love,
this anniversary night.

    —CAROL MURRAY

Many years ago, our guests of honor set sail on the sea of matrimony.
And tonight, despite a few barnacles, they're still afloat.

WHAT GREATER THING

· · · · · · · · · · · · · · · · · ·

(from *Adam Bede*)

What greater thing is there for two human souls,
than to feel that they are joined for life—
to strengthen each other in all labor,
to rest on each other in all sorrow,
to minister to each other in all pain,
to be one with each other
in silent unspeakable memories…
   —GEORGE ELIOT

Love is giving of yourself completely without feeling empty;
knowing each other fully while finding there's still more to discover.
Happy Anniversary!
   —MICHELLE HEIDENRICH BARNES

Here's to the definition of marital bliss…
knowing when to keep your lips sealed, except for a kiss!
   —SHEILA WIPPERMAN

ART & CREATIVITY

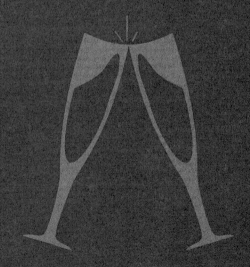

You are always on your way to a miracle.

—SARK

The world is but a canvas to our imagination.

—HENRY DAVID THOREAU

If you can dream it, you can do it.

—WALT DISNEY

To believe in the things you can see and touch is no belief at all;
but to believe in the unseen is a triumph and a blessing.

—ABRAHAM LINCOLN

Art is when you hear a knocking from your soul and you answer.

—STAR RICHÉS

Your world is vast;
your imagination infinite.
You show us our souls
by your mastered hand.

—MARY MAUDE DANIELS

BE YOU

Think outside the box.
Sing the songs unsung.
Walk where there is no path.

Be true.
Be you.

—SANDRA E. MCBRIDE

Be daring.
Take a chance!
Life is a song. Life is a dance.
Laugh. Dare to make mistakes.
Creativity is for those
who are not afraid!

—SHERRI WAAS SHUNFENTHAL

Art is the imagination
completing its mission
here on earth.
 —PAULA TIMPSON

Here's to creativity,
to paths outside our comfort zone
where each new block is not a rock,
but just a stepping stone.
 —CHARLES GHIGNA

To the artist who sees
the magic in clutter—
a cobweb,
a dust bunny,
a sheaf of papers
askew.
 —MARY MAUDE DANIELS

May you paint the sunset with your eyes,
May you sculpt the morning with your heart;
May you brush your dreams with light and laughter,
May you make your life a work of art.
 —CHARLES GHIGNA

TO ART!
· · · · · · ·

To the work of the hands,
to the vision of the mind,
to the yearning of the heart,
to creativity! To art!
—BARBARA YOUNGER

Artists are the rememberers,
the lovers and givers,
when others forget.
—JANINE CANAN

Art is undefinable,
A mystery of creation
Inspired by a pigment
Of your imagination!
—CHARLES GHIGNA

Here's to Creativity and Imagination, those magical qualities that engender renewal and rebirth. Imagination breaks the barriers of the impossible by creating the possible: the vision, the song, the novel, the poem, which, as it passes from one to another, becomes the thing itself, the thing that began its existence with the act of creative imagination. To imagine makes the unimaginable possible.

—RUTH TREESON (HOLOCAUST SURVIVOR)

Art is simply a gift—
but how passionately and totally
the artist gives it.
—JANINE CANAN

AWARD PRESENTATIONS

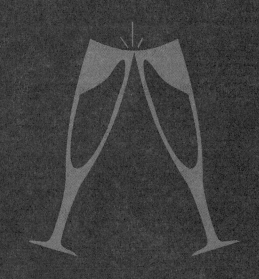

Congratulations on your achievements
from those who follow in your footsteps.
—SALLY CLARK

Isn't it good?
Ain't it grand?
The award you're holding
in your hand.
—JILL N. MACGREGOR

To fortitude and perseverance,
and the honor brought to our school [or company]—
we applaud you!
—MARY LENORE QUIGLEY

May comets streaking overhead,
dust energy into your dreams.
May your dreams
ignite your tomorrows.
—SARA SANDERSON

BABIES & CHRISTENINGS

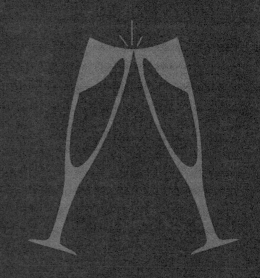

A baby is God's opinion that life should go on. Never will a time come when the most marvelous recent invention is as marvelous as a newborn baby.

—CARL SANDBURG

When I approach a child, he inspires in me two sentiments; tenderness for what he is, and respect for what he may become.

—LOUIS PASTEUR

I think, at a child's birth, if a mother could ask a fairy godmother to endow it with the most useful gift, that gift would be curiosity.

—ELEANOR ROOSEVELT

If you can give your son or daughter only one gift, let it be enthusiasm.

—BRUCE BARTON

A perfect example of minority rule is a baby in the house.

Eternal Creator,
bless _____ for
he/she is Your child.

Keep him/her with
your love. May
his/her life be

fulfilled by Your
infinite presence.
Amen.
　　　—THOMAS L. REID

To quiet nights and dry diapers!

To be blessed to have a little one
to cuddle and embrace
is the substance and the evidence
of God's amazing grace.
　　　—ANNE PENROD

THE GIFT

A child is born.
A gift to you
wrapped in heavenly blessings.
May your arms
cradle her in life.
May your voice
offer her guidance.
May your gentle touch
help her blossom.
But most of all—
may God's precious love
adorn her with wonder
and purpose.

—LESLIE A. NEILSON

A CHRISTENING BLESSING

Blessed be _____
who brings joy into the world,
whose birth gifts us with new graces,
whose very breath takes us
to new places.

Praise be the goodness
from whence such blessings flow.
Praised be all
who nurture this child,
who help her grow.

—MICHAEL S. GLASER

A DEDICATION PRAYER

Heavenly Father of Our Family,

We promise to take care of this precious child for You. We promise to pray for her. We promise to teach her Your ways and Your Word. We promise to love her as You love us.

We ask You to give us wisdom, strength, and compasssion. We ask You to protect her in every way throughout her life. We ask You to lead her into a life of loving and serving You. May she be Yours forever and be everything You intend her to be.

—ELIZABETH ADAM

A BLESSING FOR OUR CHILDREN

Blessed be our children
who take us out of ourselves,
who teach us,
even as they grow from us.
—MICHAEL S. GLASER

From this day forth, our dearest one,
our lives and hearts are intertwined.
You are our child, a gift from God,
our treasure sublime.
—ELIZABETH CAMPBELL

CHRISTENING BLESSING

Dearest God in Heaven,
Bless this child and bless this day
of new beginnings.
Smile upon this child,
and surround this child
with the soft mantle of your love.
Teach this child to follow your footsteps
and to live life in the ways of
Love, Faith, Hope, and Charity.

Be who you are—
and may you be blessed
in all that you are.

BIRTHDAYS

May you live all the days of your life.

—JONATHAN SWIFT

In youth we learn; in age, we understand.

—MARIE VON EBNER-ESCHENBACH

As soon as people are old enough to know better,
they don't know anything at all.

—OSCAR WILDE

The longer I live, the more beautiful life becomes.

—FRANK LLOYD WRIGHT

Everyone is the age of one's heart.

—GUATEMALAN PROVERB

God, grant me the Senility
to forget the people
I never liked anyway,
the good fortune
to run into the ones I do,
and the eyesight
to tell the difference.

Happy birthday to you
And many to be,
With friends that are true
As you are to me.

May you live as long as you like
and may you like as long as you live.
—BARBARA J. MITCHELL

As the heavens play out the music
of all life,
your notes are unique.
Today, we celebrate
the melody
of you.
Sing on.
    —SARA SANDERSON

May the most you wish for
be the least you get.

In every succeeding year, may you sing more than you weep.
    —ADAPTED FROM WILLIAM BUTLER YEATS

May you get it all together before you come apart.
    —BILL LEARY, QUOTED IN *READER'S DIGEST*, JUNE 1982

May you have been born on your lucky star
and may that star never lose its twinkle.

Enjoy.
Breathe deep.
Dance a little
if only in your heart.
Drink to the future
but savor the past.
Sing an old song.
Say a blessing.
Celebrate!

    —JOANNE SELTZER

LIGHT A CANDLE

Each candle on your birthday cake
shines light from a past year,
the hopes, the dreams,
the lives you've touched,
and those who hold you dear.

So light an extra candle—
make a wish for coming days,
that you be blessed with health and joy
and friends along the way.

    —DORIS SCHUCHARD

Today is yours—
    to reflect on your dreams
    to reach for the future
    to savor your individuality
    and to dance to your own rhythm.
A day to celebrate yourself,
Happy Birthday!
    —ANDREA L. MACK

BIRTHDAY BLESSING

May your leaps in life
offer wonderful opportunities.
May the love that surrounds you
forever overflow.
May your eyes rest upon
all that is good, pure, and divine.
    —ANNIE DOUGHERTY

Count your life by smiles, not tears.
Count your age by friends, not years.

BECAUSE YOU WERE BORN

On this day we celebrate
the occasion of your birth;
and express to God our gratitude
that you walk upon this earth.
—SALLY CLARK

May every day bring more happiness than yesterday.

BLESSINGS

ONE

• • •

Above and below
Outside and within
One Life
One Light
One Love
Now and forevermore
Amen

—ARLENE GAY LEVINE

Be generous in prosperity,
and thankful in adversity.
Be fair in judgment,
and guarded in your speech.
Be a lamp to those who walk in darkness,
and a home to the stranger.
Be eyes to the blind,
and a guiding light to the feet of the erring.
Be a breath of life to the body of humankind,
a dew to the soil of the human heart,
and a fruit upon the tree of humility.

—BAHA'I PRAYER, PERSIA

OUR WISH FOR YOU

May you always see beauty in the world
And hear music every day.
May you know the touch of gentle hands
And walk the peaceful way.

May the words you speak be loving,
May laughter see you through.
May you be blessed with hope and joy—
These gifts we wish for you.

—THERESA MARY GRASS

Just to be is a blessing. Just to live is holy.

—ABRAHAM HESCHEL

CELTIC BLESSING

May joy and peace surround you.
Contentment latch your door.
May happiness be with you now,
And God bless you evermore.

May you have warm words
on a cold evening,
a full moon on a dark night,
and the road downhill all the way
to your door.

WHEREVER YOU GO

May you always have
family and friends to comfort and guide you,
those you love close beside you.
May each of your days hold a golden dawn,
and may every joy linger on.
Wherever you go, may you be blessed
with all that makes you happiest.

—THERESA MARY GRASS

Go with the strength you have.
Go simply, lightly, gently,
and the Spirit go with you.

—KIAMU CAWIDRONE

May the road rise to meet you.
May the wind be always at your back.
May the sun shine warm upon your face.
And rains fall soft upon your fields.
And until we meet again,
May God hold you in the hollow of His hand.

I wish you health, I wish you wealth, and happiness galore.
I wish you luck for you and friends; what could I wish you more?
May your joys be as deep as the oceans,
your troubles as light as its foam.
And may you find, sweet peace of mind,
where ever you may roam.

May there always be work for your hands to do.
May your purse always hold a coin or two.
May the sun always shine warm on your windowpane.
May a rainbow be certain to follow each rain.
May the hand of a friend always be near you.
And may God fill your heart with gladness to cheer you.

ON THIS DAY'S ROAD

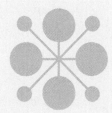

May goodness ever surround you.
May grace keep its arms around you.
May God, rich in mercy,
grant that you'll be
filled with all the love
your heart can hold
on this day's road
and forever.

—JIM CROEGAERT

May the long time sun shine upon you
all love surround you, and the pure light
within you guide you all the way on.

Now may every living thing, young or old,
weak or strong, living near or far, known or
unknown, living or departed or yet unborn,
may every living thing be full of bliss.

In the name of all those who are blessed—
Let us be a blessing.
　　—ANNIE DOUGHERTY

　　　May life protect us and surprise us
and be no more harsh than our spirits may bear.
　　　　　　　Amen.
　　—CONGREGATION OF ABRAXAS (ADAPTED)

CELEBRATION PRAYER

　　　We pray our celebration
　　　Be blessed by God above
　　With sounds of joyful laughter,
　　With warmth, and cheer, and love.
　　—SUSANNE WIGGINS BUNCH

Let us bless the flow of life
that revives us, sustains us,
and brings us to this time.
　　—MARCIA FALK

BON VOYAGE

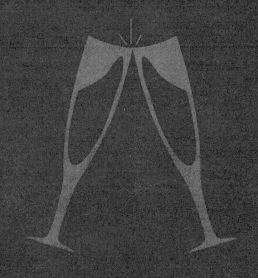

As you depart on your fabulous cruise,
may you see sights that delight and amuse—
or was it a road trip you're leaving us for?
Whatever!
We wish you adventures galore—
however, whenever, wherever you roam;
don't e-mail us photos, 'cause...
WE'RE STUCK AT HOME!
—E. SHAN CORREA

Ship to shore and back again.
May every wave be gentle
and each ripple bring a smile.
Bon Voyage!
—MARILYN HUNTMAN GIESE

We send you on your journey
with rollicking wishes for a fabulous adventure!
May you meet warm people and a proud glowing culture.
May you return to us with new stories, songs, and dances.
—DONNA WAHLERT

BUSINESS EVENTS

A toast to our abilities
to work, achieve, perform.
A toast to opportunities
to grow, improve, inform.
A toast to our successes and
the lives they will transform.

—SUSANNE WIGGINS BUNCH

Here's to our clients—
May they be ever fruitful, and multiply!

—MELISSA HED

To our success:
born from big ideas,
courageous decisions,
and dedicated teamwork.

—MELISSA HED

To all that we may
accomplish together
that we could never
achieve alone—
to teamwork!
—SALLY CLARK

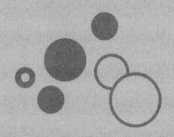

Success sparkles
from new ventures,
spontaneous ideas,
and creative light.
Thank you for making
our vision possible.
—KAREN O'LEARY

At our meeting's end,
may we still be friends!
—MARY LENORE QUIGLEY

Tonight we dine. Tomorrow we resume work. Let's all make an effort to speak with our dinner companions about topics that have nothing to do with what we do for a living. Our spouses will be pleasantly surprised. Cheers!

—JANICE A. FARRINGER

Great visions become reality
in the lives of those
who believe in themselves
and in their dreams.
Wishing you every success!

—DONNA WYLAND

Here's to having Plans B through Z
ready to save the day,
when Plan A isn't going our way.

—ERIC KOBB MILLER

CHARITY

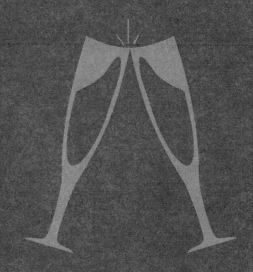

> Do your little bit of good where you are; it's those little bits of good put together that overwhelm the world.
>
> —DESMOND TUTU

> God gives us all we need,
> so we can give to others in their need.

O God, when I have food, help me to remember the hungry; when I have work, help me to remember the jobless; when I have a home, help me to remember those who have no home at all; when I am without pain, help me to remember those who suffer, and remembering, help me to destroy my complacency; bestir my compassion, and be concerned enough to help; by word and deed, those who cry out for what we take for granted.

—SAMUEL F. PUGH

May we realize that the best exercise for our heart
is bending down and lifting up others.
—THOMAS L. REID

To the act of giving—
when you sow the seeds of charity,
you reap a bountiful crop.
—BARB MAYER

A BLESSING FOR A CHARITY EVENT

It is with warmth in our hearts that we gather here today.
May our compassion steer our generous spirits in service to
(name of organization).
Let us be shepherds in this world of uncertain times.
May courage and strength guide us as we go forth with our mission.
—JUDY ACKLEY BROWN

CHILDREN

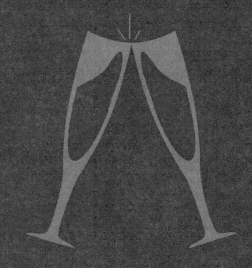

> Grown-ups never understand anything by themselves, and it is tiresome for children to be always and forever explaining things to them.
>
> —ANTOINE DE SAINT-EXUPÉRY, *THE LITTLE PRINCE*

> Always obey your parents, when they are present.
>
> —MARK TWAIN

A TOAST TO THE TOOTH FAIRY

Here's to the old tooth under the pillow,
Here's to the space that it left behind,
Here's to the new tooth soon to follow,
Here's to the tooth fairy, generous and kind!

—BARBARA YOUNGER

IN CELEBRATION OF A NEWBORN

Baby dear,
your sails are set
for the joyous trip
called life.
May you always find
brisk winds,
a guiding star,
and safe harbors.

—BARBARA J. HOLT

Let the children flourish:
dance with laughter,
dare to sing.
May you always
nourish,
praise,
encourage,
dream of Heaven,
take wing.

—DONNA AUSTGEN FRISINGER

They age us,
but keep us young.
They bring out our very worst,
and our very best,
but nothing brings greater importance to our lives,
than our children.

—DIANE M. GEISER

TO MY CHILDREN

The day you were born
the whole world sang.

The bells, touched with gladness,
incessantly rang.

The forest was bathed in the
sunset's soft glow.

In joy you were blessed
to live and to grow.

—GWEN TREMAIN RUNYARD

What gifts children are—
colorful blessings.
Every child is beautiful.
They shine as stars.
Children are light
hope
and
peace
forevermore.
—PAULA TIMPSON

A WEEPING WILLOW PRAYER

Lord, grow our children
like your willow tree
with graceful branches,
each chain bowed,
weighted with humility.
Sustain their roots in rich
firm soil, their light-green
leaves with full sunshine.
Make their shelter strong,
inviting, for hearts to hang
upon their limbs.
—NANCY TUPPER LING

CHILDREN'S BLESSINGS

Be thou a bright flame before me.
Be thou a guiding star above me.
Be thou a smooth path below me.
Be thou a kindly shepherd behind me,
today—tonight—and forever.

—SAINT COLUMBA OF IONA

May you be blessed by your dreams
and the courage to chase them.

—DIANE M. GEISER

Bless the children of the world.
May each child have shelter from the cold,
laughter to warm the heart,
honey to taste life's sweetness,
freedom to grow to potential
and knowledge of Your love.

—JO-ANNE ROWLEY

May we walk with grace
and may the light of the universe
shine upon our path.

CHILDREN'S GRACES

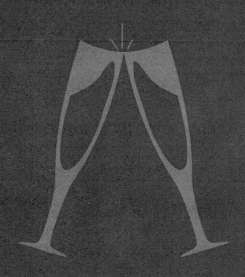

A CHILD'S GRACE

Thanks for birds that hurry by,
for fireflies flashing in the sky.

For sounds of music, chocolate s'mores,
for kitty cats and sandy shores.

For rainbows after cooling rain
and summer sunshine once again.

For misty moonlight, stars above,
for friends and families and love.
—CAROL MURRAY

Thank you for the wind and rain
and sun and pleasant weather;
thank you for this our food
and that we are together.

I love God
and God loves me.
Here's to God
and family!
—MARY LENORE QUIGLEY

Bless our soil,
so loose and light.
Bless our garden,
so green and bright.
And bless our food,
that grew just right!
—DIANE M. GEISER

Bless what we eat.
Bless us, too.
And help us remember
To always thank you.
—THERESA MARY GRASS

DEAR EARTH, DEAR SUN

Earth, who brings to us this food,
Sun, who makes it ripe and good,
Dear Earth, Dear Sun, by you we live,
Our loving thanks to you we give.

Morning, God. Time to soar!
—ANNIE DOUGHERTY

I'M THANKFUL

For rain and sun
for friends and fun,
I'm thankful.

For home and food
for all things good,
I'm thankful.

Amen.
—DEMAR REGIER

BIRTHDAY GRACE

· · · · · · · · · · · · ·

Dear God,
Before I make a wish
And blow out the candles,
I'll take a moment
To admire my cake and
To look at the faces
Around me.
Thank you for family
And thank you for friends.
Thank you for cakes
With plenty of frosting
And for one more candle
Every year.
Amen.

—BARBARA YOUNGER

Dear God,
Forgive me for stepping on a spider.
Forgive me for my mean words.
Help me to be kind to bugs and animals and friends.

—JUDY ACKLEY BROWN

MY PLACE, A TABLE GRACE

Dear God,
I'm happy to sit at my place
And thank you with this table grace
For food and laughter
And family love and all
Good gifts sent from above.
Amen.

—BARBARA YOUNGER

PRAYER IN THREE SIMPLE STEPS

1. Close your eyes.
2. Take a long, slow breath.
3. Listen: God loves you.
Amen.

—KATHRYN SCHULTZ ZERLER

For this food, for these drinks,
For shelter and for air,
Thank you, God, for all your gifts
And for your loving care.

—E. SHAN CORREA

Thank you for this yummy food.
It puts me in a happy mood.
To know that it will keep me strong
To play in God's world all day long.

—SUSAN PAURAZAS

THANKS TO THE SUN

Dear old Goldenface
we praise you
for your beaming light
for the smile of your early rises
for your laughter over the noon
for your goodnight grin

Be sure to come back tomorrow.

—JAMES BROUGHTON

HARMONY

· · · · · · ·

May all I say and all I think
be in harmony with thee,
God within me, God beyond me,
maker of the trees.

— CHINOOK PSALTER

CHILDREN'S TOASTS

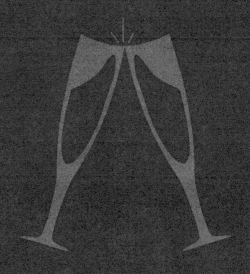

TRADITIONAL JEWISH TOAST

To Life!

A HOT CHOCOLATE TOAST

(You may toast outdoors or inside.)

To the winter night!
Bold. Cold. Starry. Bright.
We raise our mugs,
and take a sip,
and welcome warmth,
up to our lips.
—BARBARA YOUNGER

If I could search the world around,
true comfort for my heart be found;
I know what I would love the best,
it is my parents' arms for rest.
—NANCY TUPPER LING

Here's
to having
fun on
our
journey
around
the
sun.

—THOMAS L. REID

A TOAST TO SPRING

Bumblebees buzz,
Mockingbirds sing;
Hummingbirds hum—
Welcome Spring!
—CHARLES GHIGNA

A TOAST TO SUMMER

Backyard sprinklers
In the sun;
Puddles full of
Summer fun!
—CHARLES GHIGNA

A TOAST TO AUTUMN

Pumpkins smile,
Owls call;
Trick-or-treaters
Welcome Fall!
—CHARLES GHIGNA

A TOAST TO WINTER

Snowmen smile,
Gifts appear;
Choirs sing—
Winter's here!
—CHARLES GHIGNA

CLASS REUNIONS

THEN AND NOW

· · · · · · · · · · · ·

To the classmates who
knew us then and
who know us now.

May there be many more
years ahead for us to
celebrate our friendships.

—SALLY CLARK

We've come together to remember, to connect, to be one for all and
all for one; to sing the silly school song and tell stories of tests and
teachers, victories and losses, games and plays. Let's celebrate our
refusal to believe you can't go home again. Turns out you can—
because we have! Salute!

—MARTHA K. BAKER

Have fun, relax,
remember the past.
Here's to our class…
the years sure went fast.

—DONNA WYLAND

Despite months and miles away,
it's like we never parted.
The happiness of the future dwells
in memories of yesterdays.
—JAMES PENHA

Like rings of a tree
each year, each storm,
each wrinkle and roll,
the hard times and good
have brought strength to our roots;
they've helped us stand tall—
to find pride in whom
we've become.
To us!
—MICHELLE CLOSE MILLS

Here's to everyone from our graduating class;
it's so wonderful to see you all again!
You look as great as you did in high school—
so glad I left my glasses at home. Cheers!
—CAROLE BLAKE

To everyone here today, welcome.
To those unable to make the journey, you are missed.
And to our dearly departed who are forever in our hearts.
—MARY LENORE QUIGLEY

To our friends who made school fun.
To our teachers who made it interesting.
And to our parents who made it necessary.
—NORMAN STYERS

FAMILY

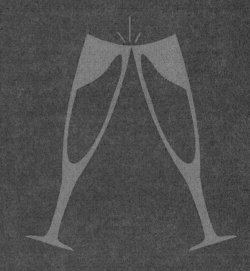

> One hundred years from now, it will not matter what my bank account was, how big my house was, or what kind of car I drove. But the world may be a little better, because I was important in the life of a child.
>
> —FOREST WITCRAFT

> Where thou art—that—is Home.
>
> —EMILY DICKINSON

PEACE IN OUR HOMES

May our words be gentle,
our actions loving,
our intentions honorable…
for a peaceful world can be created only
by those who practice peace,
each moment of each day
in their hearts and in their homes.

—CAROLINE JOY ADAMS

Gentle God,
grant that at home
when we are most truly ourselves,
where we are known at our best and worst,
we may learn to forgive and be forgiven.

—A NEW ZEALAND PRAYER BOOK

A BLESSING FOR FAMILY

May our family be blessed with comforts of the physical
  and riches of the spirit.
May our paths be lit with sunshine
  and sorrow ne'er darken our doors.
May our harvest be bountiful
  and our hearth ever welcoming.
May we celebrate together in times of joy
  and comfort one another in times of sorrow.
And mostly:
may we always stay together
  and share the laughter, the love, and the tears
   as only family can.
 —DANIELLE BRIGANTE

Bricks and mortar make a house,
but the laughter of children
makes a home.
Here's to family!
 —IRISH PROVERB

As an Albanian proverb says,
the sun at home warms better
than the sun elsewhere.
Here's to our home and family!

Let us raise our glasses
and then drink up
to the greatest of folks
who reared us up!

IN CELEBRATION OF THE FAMILY

Join and bless this family, O God, so that its circle be where quarrels are made up; where errors are forgiven and solutions found. Family is where we first find love, acceptance, security; where we are first celebrated and cherished. Keep our home fires burning; You, O God, are the fuel from which we gain warmth, safety, and inspiration.

—MARGARET ANNE HUFFMAN

May the family ties that bind us,
leave us forever thankful
for hearts of homegrown love.
—ANNE CALODICH FONE

FAMILY REUNIONS

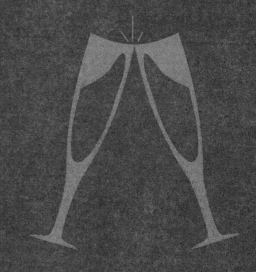

> A family is the soil from which
> we have grown and travel far beyond,
> bearing the fruits of the seeds
> we carry with us.
> —SALLY CLARK

FAMILY RE-UNION

. . . .

We come together
one yet many;
each from
a different path
to an intersection
of time and memory.
We travel under
the same sky
brilliant with stars,
sleep beneath
the changing moon.
We will leave
not as strangers,
but as pilgrims
on this rich earth.

—ANNE SPRING

THE PERFECT CHORD

The diversity in the family should be the cause of love and harmony,
as it is in music where many different notes
blend together in the making of a perfect chord.
　—FROM THE BAHA'I SCRIPTURES, PERSIA

COUNTING BLESSINGS

Let this day warm our hearts and lift our spirits.
Let this night bring dreams of moon-kissed memories.
Let these blessings embrace and protect us
as we give thanks for our family,
bound by ties of unconditional love.
　—JUDITH A. LINDBERG

FAMILIES REMEMBER

Families remember who we were,
see who we are now,
and know how we got there;
forever a part of our history,
the root of all our dreams.

—SALLY CLARK

BEGINNINGS

Though the winds of life will
blow us all in different directions,
may we always return to
the place where we started
and to the people we love.

—SALLY CLARK

FORTUNE
& PROSPERITY

It is only with gratitude that life becomes rich.

—DIETRICH BONHOEFFER

I followed the river and it led to the Ocean.

—JANINE CANAN

I do want to get rich but I never want to do what there is to do to get rich.

—GERTRUDE STEIN

Here's to a full belly, a heavy purse, and a light heart!

Raise your glass,
and I'll raise mine—
to future success.
Now drink your wine.
Cheers!
—BENITA GLICKMAN

In the garden of life, may your pea pods never be empty.

—BILL COPELAND

Here's to fortune and prosperity. To our families, our loved ones, our friends—these are the things in life that enrich us and help us through good times and bad times. Money and material possessions come and go, but those who are nearest and dearest stand by us forever.

—BARB MAYER

OUR MANY BLESSINGS

When we count our many blessings,
It isn't hard to see,
That life's most valued treasures
Are the treasures that are free.
For it isn't what we own or buy
That signifies our wealth,
It's the special gifts that have no price:
Our family, friends and health.
May Your Blessings Be Many!

It is said that one man's misfortune is another man's gain. Let's prove the cynics wrong. By sharing our fortune and prosperity with those less fortunate, we can create a chain of prosperity that will travel to infinity. Here's to the giving!

—BARB MAYER

May you prosper every day!

—MARY LENORE QUIGLEY

May our hunger be sated.
Our thirst be quenched.
When it's raining money
Here's hoping we're drenched!

—MELISSA HED

TO YOUR SUCCESS

May all your decisions
be the right ones made
with wisdom and courage;
may good fortune be the seed you plant
and prosperity the crop you harvest.

—SALLY CLARK

The world is jeweled in all directions,
no matter where you are,
you stand in great beauty and truth.
To wealth—
and to life!
   —RAMNATH SUBRAMANIAN

Here's to our creditors—may they be endowed
with the three virtues, faith, hope, and charity.

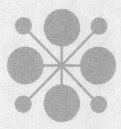

FRIENDSHIP

No love, no friendship, can cross the path of our destiny without leaving some mark on it forever.

—FRANÇOIS MAURIAC

My best friend is one who brings out the best in me.

—HENRY FORD

One of the most beautiful qualities of true friendship is to understand and be understood.

—SENECA

I drink to your charm, your beauty and your brains— which gives you a rough idea of how hard up I am for a drink.

—GROUCHO MARX

TO FRIENDSHIP

Here is to friendship
    that spans years
    that spans distance
    that spans change.

Here is to friendship
    that sees flaws and
    does not note them but
    for the humor they provide,
    the humanity they reveal.

Here is to friendship
    that not only survives
    but thrives amidst and against
    the ravages of time; that knows loss but
    knows a bond that has held
    and will hold.

Here is to friendship!
    —JIM CROEGAERT

May we treat our friends with kindness—
and our enemies with generosity.

The Lord gives us our relatives.
Thank God we can choose our friends.
—ETHEL WATTS MUMFORD

To our best friends,
who know the worst about us
but refuse to believe it.

The gift of your friendship
is something I would never exchange.
—JANET LOMBARD

Heart to heart,
friend to friend,
beloved ever real.
The truest tithe my heart can give
is the grace of loving you.
   —MARY MAUDE DANIELS

WHAT A JOY TO JOIN TOGETHER

What a joy to join together,
And break a loaf of bread.
What a joy in friends abiding,
And sharing what is fed.

Embracing and enfolding
The breath of every life,
All in celebration
Of what is good and right.
— ANNIE DOUGHERTY

To friends—as long as we are able
to lift our glasses from the table!

There are good ships, and wood ships,
and ships that sail the sea,
but the best ships are friendships
and may they always be.

THE HUMAN TOUCH

'Tis the human touch in this world that counts,
    the touch of your hand and mine,
which means far more to the fainting heart
    than shelter and bread and wine;
for shelter is gone when the night is o'er
    and bread lasts only a day,
but the touch of the hand and the sound of the voice
    sings on in the soul always.
—SPENCER MICHAEL FREE

A FRIENDSHIP TOAST

To your good health, old friend.
May you live for a thousand years,
    and I be there to count them.
—ROBERT SMITH SURTEES

May friendship, like wine, improve as time advances.
And may we always have old wine, old friends, and young cares.

A friend is one that knows you as you are,
understands where you have been,
accepts what you have become,
and still, gently allows you to grow.

Friends...
They cherish one another's hopes.
They are kind to one another's dreams.
    —HENRY DAVID THOREAU

GENERAL TOASTS

> Wine makes a man more pleased with himself;
> I do not say that it makes him more pleasing to others.
> —SAMUEL JOHNSON

For every wound, a balm,
for every sorrow, a cheer.
For every storm, a calm,
for every thirst, a beer.

May your days be many,
your troubles be few,
your loved ones safe,
and your friends all true.
—BARBARA BOOTHE LOYD

May gratitude at night
bring you morning delight!
—JUNE COTNER

GRATITUDE
· · · · · · · · ·

To our
friends who have become family
and our
family who have become friends—
may you be as blessed
as you've made us.

    —MARY MAUDE DANIELS

Dance as if no one were watching,
sing as if no one were listening,
and live every day as if it were your last.

Here's to our humor being wry,
our wine dry,
and our tears the cry of laughter.

    —ERIC KOBB MILLER

Hooray for the Inevitable with an extra hip hip for Love and Folly!

—JAMES BROUGHTON

May your life be long and happy,
Your cares and sorrows few;
And the many friends around you
Prove faithful, fond, and true.

Life is not measured by the number of breaths we take,
but by the moments that take our breath away.

Let every moment be filled with eternity.

—JANINE CANAN

Here's to change—
sometimes good,
and other times regrettable,
but always inevitable.

—ERIC KOBB MILLER

For all that has been—Thanks!
For all that shall be—Yes!
—DAG HAMMARSKJÖLD

A thousand days like today!

INUIT TOAST

May you have warmth in your igloo,
oil in your lamp,
and peace in your heart.

GRACES

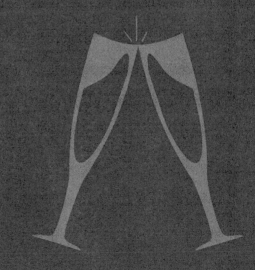

FRIENDSHIP GRACE

· · · · · · · · · · · · ·

Dearest God, loving and loyal provider of our daily bread, we welcome you to our table. We thank you for this beautiful gathering of friends. We ask you to bless this bread and share it with us today. You are the leaven for our endeavors and the source of our strength. With sweet voices of praise and thanksgiving, we ready ourselves to share and celebrate the wonders of this day just the way you would have us do. Amen.

—ANNIE DOUGHERTY

We thank Great Spirit for the resources that made this food possible;
we thank the Earth Mother for producing it,
and we thank all those who labored to bring it to us.
May the Wholesomeness of the food before us,
bring out the Wholesomeness of the Spirit within us.

—NATIVE AMERICAN PRAYER

A GRACE OF CARE

May this food that feeds my body,
also nourish you.
May this love that lives within me,
likewise dwell in you.

—LICIA RANDO

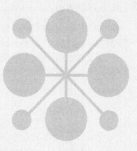

Heal us.
Lift us.
Stir us.
Gift us.
Let us be a blessing
and a reflection of You.
Amen.

—DEBORAH GORDON COOPER

A BUDDHIST GRACE

• • • • • • • • • • • •

(In Buddhist monasteries before every meal,
a monk or a nun recites these Five Contemplations.)

This food is the gift of the whole universe— the earth, the sky, and
much hard work. May we live in a way that is worthy of this food. May we
transform our unskillful states of mind, especially that of greed. May
we eat only foods that nourish us and prevent illness. May we accept this
food for the realization of the way of understanding and love.

For each new morning with its light,
for rest and shelter of the night,
for health and food,
for love and friends,
for everything Thy goodness sends.
    —RALPH WALDO EMERSON

IRISH GRACE

May this food restore our strength, giving new energy to tired limbs, new thoughts to weary minds. May this drink restore our soul, giving new vision to dry spirits, new warmth to cold hearts. And once refreshed, may we give new pleasure to You, who gives us all.

GRACE FOR A GATHERING

Bless our family with peace and joy,
let our words to each other be kind,
and our actions gentle.
May the love that we share be *your* love,
so that each of us can always say:
Lord, it is good for us to be here!
—ANYA CARA

May God bless
our meal and grant us a
compassionate and understanding heart
toward one another.
—MOUNT ST. MARY'S ABBEY,
WRENTHAM, MASSACHUSETTS

A GRACE FOR FRIENDS

Traveler…be at peace.

You are welcome here.

Our door is open.

Hands extend across the table.

Bread is broken in shared contentment.

Hearts are warmed and healed anew.

Let this house

be a harbor in breeze or gale.

Traveler…fair winds be at your sail.

—STEPHEN KOPEL

GRADUATIONS

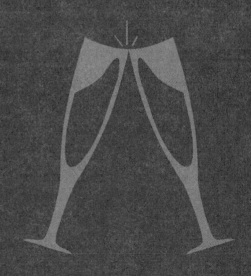

Always do right. That will gratify some of the people, and astonish the rest.

—MARK TWAIN

What we become is more important than where we're from.

What we learn we learn by doing.

—ARISTOTLE

Learn from the past.
Prepare for the future.
Make the most of today.
—SHEILA WIPPERMAN

TO REACH
· · · · · · · ·

As you step,
one foot before the other,
remember to reach—
not just for the stars,
but to touch another's heart.
　　—ANNIE DOUGHERTY

To Mom and Dad
who have helped me so far,
may I ask one small favor?
The keys to the car.

Do not go where the path may lead.
Go instead where there is no path
and leave a trail.
　　—RALPH WALDO EMERSON

A TOAST TO YOUR LIFE'S JOURNEY

May you find
the way
to your heart's
true desire
and shine
your brightest light
on the way
to meet it.

— JOAN NOËLDECHEN

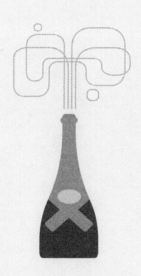

THE ANSWER

be full of joy
have a grateful heart
enjoy the journey

rejoice
always expect miracles
be thankful

let your spirit soar
be honest
embrace peace

learn to reach out
believe
nurture your soul

laugh out loud
have faith
find your way home.
—LORI EBERHARDY

A TOAST TO THE GRADUATE

Here's to a future...
inspired by dreams,
tested by challenges,
strengthened by success,
and achieved through hard work.
Congratulations!

 —ANNETTE GULATI

My dear,
on this remarkable day,
I wish for you a life filled
with health, happiness, and great meaning.
And may you continue to live a life
that inspires all of us to be our best selves.

 —MELISSA HED

To my parents.
Thank you for your support,
your help, and most of all, your money.
I fully intend to pay back the support and help.

You've earned your degree.
You've made the grade.
Success will be yours
once your loans are paid.

  —JILL N. MACGREGOR

   To all the milestones
   passed along the path
   to this new destination;
   congratulations today
   as you follow your dreams.

  —CHARMAINE PAPPAS DONOVAN

Here's to flinging
that mortarboard cap:
your past—gone with the wind—
your future—up in the air.

  —DEMAR REGIER

Now is the time to begin,
unafraid to venture into the world.
Take it by surprise with all
your energy and ideas.
Begin to build something new,
something astounding,
something your very own.
The world is waiting for you!

—SHERRI WAAS SHUNFENTHAL

One small step can transform
the world in great ways.
May all of your future steps
be world-changing.
—ANNETTE GULATI

MILESTONE

• • • • • • • •

A milestone in your life,
an ending and a beginning;
a passage that marks a new page,
waiting to be turned.
Be bold! Go forward with joy!

—SALLY CLARK

PHILOSOPHY

Be a seeker of visions—
and a hunter of dreams.
Be alert and excited
and proud of your life.
Dance with all music
and sing with all songs.
Be awestruck with wonder
and inspired by nature.
Shun what is wrong;
show wisdom and class.
Honor each promise;
love friend and foe.
Laugh with the happy
and cry with the sad—
live for tomorrow—
but save yesterday.
Run with the wind
and savor the moment.

—JOAN STEPHEN

LOOK TO THIS DAY

Look to this day,
for it is life,
the very life of life.
In its brief course lie all
the realities and verities of existence,
the bliss of growth,
the splendor of action,
the glory of power—

for yesterday is but a dream,
and tomorrow is only a vision,
but today, well lived,
makes every yesterday a dream of happiness
and every tomorrow a vision of hope.

—SANSKRIT PROVERB

GUESTS & HOSTS

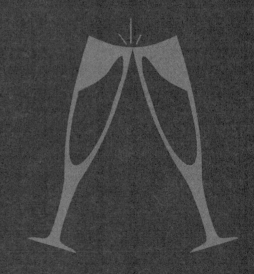

> One cannot have too large a party.
>
> —JANE AUSTEN

> Who practices hospitality entertains God himself.
>
> —PROVERB

TO OUR HOSTS:

Happiness, health, and prosperity!

TO OUR GUESTS:

Welcome to our home
may the wine warm you
may the food fill you
may joy and laughter engage you
may love surround you.

    —DONNA WAHLERT

At your table or in your home,
time spent with you is always
the perfect refreshment.

 —SALLY CLARK

Here's to our food for thought being haute cuisine
and our reasoning seasoned with common sense.

 —ERIC KOBB MILLER

A TOAST TO OUR GUESTS

May our paths always intersect,
and may our hearts always beat together.

 —JUDY ACKLEY BROWN

HAPPINESS

> A good laugh is sunshine in the house.
> —WILLIAM MAKEPEACE THACKERAY

> Happiness is a place between too little and too much.
> —FINNISH PROVERB

> Happiness takes a risk, misery plays it safe.
> —JAMES BROUGHTON

> A smile is a light in the window of the soul
> indicating that the heart is at home.

Here's to *que sera sera*
and hoping it brings lots of ha-ha-ha.
—ERIC KOBB MILLER

May we know
that more important
than what we have
is what we are,
what we do,
what we become.
  —THOMAS L. REID

Here's to singing the song in our heart, even if we can't carry a tune:
just duet.
  —ERIC KOBB MILLER

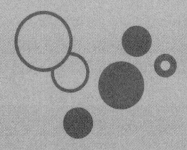

HEALTH

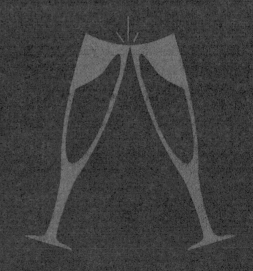

Eat, drink, and be merry for tomorrow you diet.
—SCOTTISH PROVERB

Take this life and use it.
Take this body
and strengthen it.
Take this heart
and open it.
—JANINE CANAN

May your feet never ache
and your back stay strong.
May your bones never creak
while your years grow long.
—SYLVIA FORBES

To health that flows through you
like a strong rushing stream!
To health—let it lead you
to each of your dreams!
—ANNE CALODICH FONE

HOMECOMING

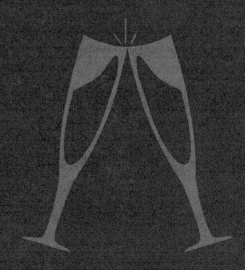

> There is nothing like staying at home, for real comfort.
> —JANE AUSTEN

> Home is the place where it feels right
> to walk around without shoes.

Our hearts are full.
Our lives are blessed.
To have you home
words can't express.
  —JILL N. MACGREGOR

May the Light shine on wherever you roam,
illuminating the way to guide you home.
  —ARLENE GAY LEVINE

You were always in our hearts and minds...
Now, at last, in our arms once more.
  —ARLENE GAY LEVINE

Home never leaves your heart,
no matter where you've been.
Welcome home, Brave Soldier!
—NANCY TUPPER LING

No matter how long ago
We walked through these doors,
Our thankful hearts remember
That we are home!
—MARY LENORE QUIGLEY

May the path of life lead you on many exciting adventures. Walk confidently through each door the world opens for you, and let the journey lead you farther than your dreams. And when your feet grow weary and your soul seeks rest, may the path wind lovingly, always, home.
—NANCY TANDON

HOUSEWARMING

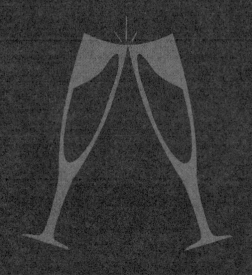

> Home is home, be it ever so humble.
> —ENGLISH PROVERB

> A house is made of walls and beams;
> a home is built with love and dreams.

> Home wasn't built in a day.
> —JANE SHERWOOD ACE

May this house be filled
with joy in the morning
and sweet dreams at night.
May it be a home
where love has come to live.

BLESS THIS HOUSE

Bless this house
    as we come and go;
Bless our home
    as the children grow;
Bless our families
    as they gather in;
Bless this house
    with love and friends.

A HOUSE BLESSING

May your home be blessed with joy
and spiced with laughter great.
May it burst its seams with love;
and memories to make.

—MARY MAUDE DANIELS

A HOUSEWARMING TOAST

May the warmth of all us gathered
toast a new address:
please lift a glass
to celebrate
a newly feathered nest.
—MARY MAUDE DANIELS

MEMORIALS & FUNERALS

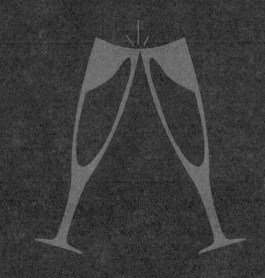

Because I could not stop for Death—
He kindly stopped for me.
—EMILY DICKINSON

Between grief and nothing I will take grief.
—WILLIAM FAULKNER

It is natural to die as to be born...
—FRANCIS BACON

The time is gone—
Slipped away...
What remains
Lays gently,
Sweetly,
Dearly,
Within the heart.
—ANNIE DOUGHERTY

Nothing is ever wholly lost.
That which is excellent
remains forever a part of this universe.
  —RALPH WALDO EMERSON

Today we gather in memory of _____
may we remember her caring and compassion
her joyful generosity
her unique creativity
her easy laugh
her selflessness
her grit and determination
her courage and strength
her faithfulness.
May we always remain faithful to her memory
and those virtues which she wore so honestly.
  —DONNA WAHLERT

(You may substitute other qualities to create
a memory of your own loved one.)

This present day.
This absent one.
We are gathered to remember
_____,
gone from view,
not from heart.
Grant a safe passage
from this earth
of wild beauty
to places unknown.
Give to those
who are left—
time to mourn,
time to heal,
and time to reflect
on the memory
of the love we shared.

 —ANNE SPRING

The body is gone,
but the love is not;
wherever we go in our lives,
for as long as we live,
_____'s life will always go
with us in our hearts.

　　—SALLY CLARK

SPLENDOR IN THE GRASS

Though nothing can bring back
the hour of splendor in the grass,
of glory in the flower;
we will grieve not,
rather find strength
in what remains behind.

　　—WILLIAM WORDSWORTH

MEMORIAL PRAYER

. . . .

Source of Life,
Spirit of Compassion,
we give thanks,
from the fullness of our hearts,
for the life that we remember
in this gathering.
Let the meaning of her/his life
live on in us.
May the light that she/he has given us
shine on in our own lives
and hearts and memories.
Help us to find the courage
and the faith
we need each day
to carry on.
Open a way of hope before us.
Mend our hearts and teach us
to be comforters
of one another.

—DEBORAH GORDON COOPER

Death is nothing at all:
I have only slipped away into the next room.
I am I and you are you;
whatever we were to each other, that we are still.
Call me by my old familiar name,
speak to me in the easy way which you always used.
Put no difference in your tone;
wear no forced air or solemnity or sorrow.
Laugh as we always laughed at the little jokes we enjoyed together.
Play, smile, think of me, pray for me.
Why should I be out of mind because I am out of sight?
I am but waiting for you, for an interval, somewhere very near,
just around the corner.
All is well.

   —CANON HENRY SCOTT HOLLAND

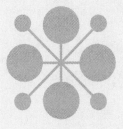

NEW JOB

A journey of a thousand miles begins with a single step.

—LAO TZU

The world is full of willing people,
some willing to work,
the rest willing to let them.

—ROBERT FROST

Here's to a future...
inspired by dreams,
tested by challenges,
strengthened by success,
and achieved through hard work.
Congratulations!

—ANNETTE GULATI

May good things and blessings happen your way,
as you start a new path in your future today.

—JILL N. MACGREGOR

In your new position,
here's to good luck, fortune,
and making a difference where it counts.
Cheers!

— PAULA E. KIRMAN

PATRIOTIC TOASTS

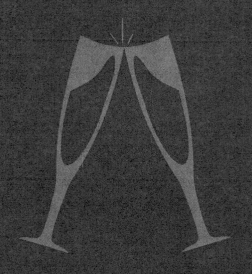

> Where liberty dwells, there is my country.
>
> —BENJAMIN FRANKLIN

Old Glory: May her stars shine forever in the eternal blue,
and her stripes reach round the world in peace!
To the soldier who fights
for the ideals of the free!
  —LOUISE I. WEBSTER

To our flag striped with red
and blazoned with stars;
to lives stitched into her history
and the freedom within her folds.
  —SALLY CLARK

You're a grand old flag,
you're a high flying flag
and forever in peace may you wave.
You're the emblem of
the land I love.
The home of the free and the brave.
  —GEORGE M. COHAN

PETS

> Animals are such agreeable friends—
> they ask no questions, they pass no criticisms.
> —GEORGE ELIOT

Welcome, new kitten,
for sure, we are smitten!
—BARBARA YOUNGER

PUPPY LOVE

Hello puppy swishy tail
shaking like a fluffy sail,
welcome our new furry friend
waving with your other end!
—CHARLES GHIGNA

AT THE GRAVE OF A FINE CAT

May your whiskers be ruffled by only pleasant breezes,
may your bowls be filled with tuna and sweet cream,
may your dreams be blessed with legions of mice,
and most of all, may you forever purr in peace.
Amen.

—BARBARA YOUNGER

BLESSING AT A PET BURIAL

Sleep well, (name of pet).
Let the earth enfold you.
Your loving spirit remains forever in our hearts.
Your playful paws will always walk beside us.
Sleep well, dearest (name of pet).

—JUDY ACKLEY BROWN

A TOAST TO OLD DOGS

Here's to old dogs,
their eyes thick with clouds,
and their beards snowy white.
Their dreams may have faded,
(they'll never catch that squirrel now),
but their love stays the same.
   —LICIA RANDO

A toast to our furry companions
who make the journey joyful,
leaving paw prints on our souls.
   —JUDY BARNES

RAINBOW BRIDGE

● ● ● ● ● ● ● ● ● ● ● ●

Just this side of heaven is a place called Rainbow Bridge. When an animal dies that has been especially close to someone here, they go to Rainbow Bridge. There are meadows and hills for all of our special friends so they can run and play together. There is plenty of food, water, and sunshine, and our friends are warm and comfortable.

All the animals who have been ill and old are restored to health and vigor; and those who were hurt or maimed are made whole and strong again, just as we remember them in our dreams of days and times gone by. The animals are happy and content, except for one small thing; they each miss someone very special to them, who had to be left behind.

They all run and play together, but the day comes when one suddenly stops and looks into the distance. His bright eyes are intent; his eager body begins to quiver. Suddenly he begins to run from the group, flying over the green grass, his legs carrying him faster and faster. You have been spotted, and when you and your special friend finally meet, you cling together in joyous reunion, never to be parted again. The happy kisses rain upon your face; your hands again caress the beloved head, and you look once more into the trusting eyes of your pet, so long gone from your life but never absent from your heart.

Then you cross Rainbow Bridge together.

RETIREMENT

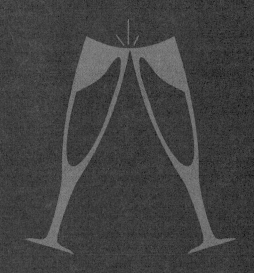

> It's better to wear out than to rust out.
>
> —BISHOP HORNE

> Retirement at sixty-five is ridiculous.
> When I was sixty-five I still had pimples.
>
> —GEORGE BURNS

THE TASTE OF SUCCESS

Released to enjoy the fruits of your labor;
to taste sweet, contented days,
to savor the joy of favorite pursuits,
to relish the friendships you've created over a lifetime.
Enjoy the feast of your retirement!

—SALLY CLARK

A TOAST FOR NEW BEGINNINGS

May you dare to live dangerously
in pursuit of what you love,

May you travel adventurously
and with vigilant curiosity,

May you sleep unfettered by agendas
of things not done,

and wake enthusiastically,
ready to embrace

your new tomorrows.

—MICHAEL S. GLASER

Every end is a beginning,
another mountain to climb
or space to pursue new possibilities, or withdraw
to the other side of the bank
under a great sprawling sycamore
where the river quietly flows
and just breathe.

   —MARIAN OLSON

> You've put in your time.
> You've paid your dues.
> From this moment on
>   it's all about you!
> —JILL N. MACGREGOR

Retirement—
just a curious word to say
you are free to do as you please;
taste new beginnings,
dream new dreams.
Be happy.

   —ZORAIDA RIVERA MORALES

WE HONOR YOU

We're grateful for what you have been and done,
and for all you are today.
We honor you with hearts of love,
as we send you on your way.
Happy retirement!

—DONNA WYLAND

Retirement means "taking back." Rediscover your freedom; your long, lazy mornings and afternoon walks. Find those things you've always wanted to do and do them.

—BARB MAYER

ENJOY YOUR REWARD

Toss the alarm clock, sell your suits,
take a vacation, count your "loot,"
but don't be lazy. You'll get bored.
We're going to miss you.
Enjoy your reward!

—DONNA WYLAND

WEDDINGS

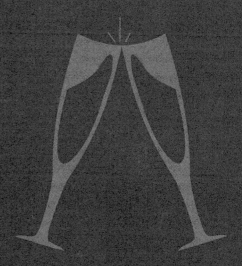

A great marriage is not when the "perfect couple" comes together. It is when an imperfect couple learns to enjoy their differences.

—DAVE MEURER

A successful marriage requires falling in love many times, always with the same person.

—MIGNON MCLAUGHLIN

When you realize you want to spend the rest of your life with someone, you want forever to start as soon as possible.

—FROM *WHEN HARRY MET SALLY*

Married couples who love each other tell each other a thousand things without talking.

—CHINESE PROVERB

We attract hearts by the qualities we display. We retain them by the qualities we possess.

—JEAN SUARD

Here's to marriage—the last decision you'll be allowed to make!

Here's to the bride,
Here's to the groom,
Here's to a wonderful honeymoon!
—SALLY CLARK

Grow old along with me!
The best is yet to be,
the last of life, for which the first was made:
our times are in his hand…
—ROBERT BROWNING

Now a husband,
Now a wife,
In joy may you live your wedded life!
—SALLY CLARK

Much happiness to the newlyweds from the oldyweds!

A NEWLYWED'S TOAST

May today's love burn brightly,
and many years from now,
may your hearts be warmed
by the glow of a flame
that never died.

—SALLY CLARK

A WEDDING BLESSING

To (bride's name) _____ and (groom's name) _____, may your journey together be strengthened by unconditional love and harmony.

May the sharing of your lives and friendship be a comfort and a blessing to one another.

May your union deeply honor the compassion and wisdom of all life and be seeded within your heart.

And may your lives together continue to unfold beautifully for all eternity.

—REVEREND PHYLLIS ANN MIN

FROM THE BRIDE'S FATHER

I toast on behalf of myself,
and I toast on behalf of my spouse.
We're glad you married our daughter,
and got her out of the house.

A WEDDING TOAST

May your
love have depth
and beauty.

May it
know that sacred
glory of

"I in you, and
you in me."
—THOMAS L. REID

Because I love you truly,
Because you love me, too,
My very greatest happiness
Is sharing life with you.

A FRIEND'S WEDDING TOAST

Here's to this fine couple.
May their joys be as bright as the morning,
and their sorrows but shadows that fade
in the sunlight of love.

A MARRIAGE FOR ALL SEASONS

May your love be as invigorating as the air of autumn.
As persevering as the winter's cold.
As refreshing as the return of spring.
And as gratifying as the fullness of summer.
May your marriage be blessed abundantly on your wedding day
and continue to grow through all the seasons of your love.

—JAN DUNLAP

May you both live as long as you want,

and never want as long as you live.

PAIUTE WEDDING PRAYER

Now you will feel no rain,

for each of you will be shelter to the other.

Now you will feel no cold,

for each of you will be warmth to the other.

Now there is no more loneliness.

Now you are two persons,

but there is only one life before you.

Go now to your dwelling place,

to enter into the days of your togetherness,

and may your days be good and long upon this earth.

SECOND MARRIAGE

We came late together, O God of second chances, making the discovery of our love even sweeter. We honor all that has brought us to this moment, trusting in Your promise to make all things new. Give us many years to share so that we can weave them together with vibrant strands of loyalty, kindness, and warmth into a coverlet of married love, a wedding gift from You.

—MARGARET ANNE HUFFMAN

SOUL MATES

The quiet miracle
of a man and woman
uniting as one,
to travel the road of happy destiny
together,
is like a sacred haven in the sky,
the feeling of having arrived
without ever leaving.

—JENNIFER M. SPENCER

May brooks and trees and singing hills
Join in the chorus, too.
And every gentle wind that blows
Send happiness to you.

From this day forward,
you shall not walk alone.
My heart will be your shelter,
and my arms will be your home.

When the roaring flames of your love
have burned down to embers,
may you find that you've married
your best friend.

PARENTS' TOAST

When children find true love,
parents find true joy.
Here's to you two,
may your joy and ours last forever.

May your hands be forever clasped in friendship
and your hearts joined forever in love.

grow always
grow together
find your music
and dance
—GAAR SCOTT

BLESSING THE BELOVED

. . . .

One partner: How fine
                         you are, my love,
                         how fine you are.

The other partner: How fine
                         are you, my love,
                         what joy is ours.

Together: Of all pleasure,
                         how sweet
                         is the taste of love.
—AFTER SONG OF SONGS 1:15-16, 7:7

To the joining of hands
the uniting of hearts
the blending of paths
never to part.
—LOUISE I. WEBSTER

The goal of marriage is to give the best years of your life
to the spouse who *makes* them the best years of your life.

A TOAST FROM THE BRIDE AND GROOM
TO ONE ANOTHER:

It is the true season of love when we know that we alone can love;
that no one could ever have loved before us and that no one will
ever love in the same way after us.

—JOHANN WOLFGANG VON GOETHE

My bounty is as boundless as the sea.
My love as deep. The more I give to thee,
the more I have, for both are infinite.

—WILLIAM SHAKESPEARE

This is my beloved, and this is my friend.

—SONG OF SOLOMON 5:16

HOW DO I LOVE THEE? SONNET 43

How do I love thee? Let me count the ways.
I love thee to the depth and breadth and height
My soul can reach, when feeling out of sight
For the ends of being and ideal grace.
I love thee to the level of every day's
Most quiet need, by sun and candle-light.
I love thee freely, as men strive for right.
I love thee purely, as they turn from praise.
I love thee with the passion put to use
In my old griefs, and with my childhood's faith.
I love thee with a love I seemed to lose
With my lost saints. I love thee with the breath,
Smiles, tears, of all my life; and, if God choose,
I shall but love thee better after death.

—ELIZABETH BARRETT BROWNING

A TOAST TO PARENTS

. . . .

There is no more lovely, friendly, and charming relationship, communion or company than a good marriage.

—MARTIN LUTHER

(Follow this with lively reflections on how your parents' marriage inspired you.)

May the two of you grow old on one pillow.

Here's to matrimony, the high sea for which
no compass has yet been invented.

—HEINRICH HEINE

ON YOUR WEDDING DAY

Today—
embrace the melody
of your love.
Share the beauty
of your song
and never, ever stop singing.

—LESLIE A. NEILSON

May this, your day, be special.
May your lives and vows be blest.
May the future you build together
Be filled with all God's best!

—JILL N. MACGREGOR

HOLIDAYS

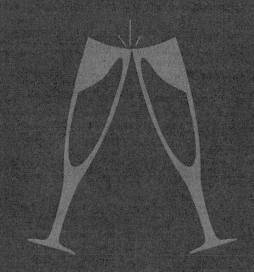

NEW YEAR

Ring out the old, ring in the new,
Ring, happy bells, across the snow:
The year is going, let him go;
Ring out the false, ring in the true.

—ALFRED, LORD TENNYSON

TOAST TO THE NEW YEAR

May our hearts be ever thankful
as we honor this New Year,
for the bounty of our blessings,
new bright hopes to bring good cheer.

—NORMA WOODBRIDGE

PRAISE FOR THE NEW YEAR

Welcome in the New Year
as you would a friend;
one who brings twelve shining gifts
to last until year's end.
Harmony with others,
faith in each new day;
all the kindness you can spare,
goodwill in words you say.
Compassion for earth's creatures,
and hope for those in need;
make peace with all of nature,
make tolerance your creed.
Thoughtfulness and sharing,
love spread far and near;
a thankfulness for living
to end a perfect year.

—SHEILA FORSYTH

We toast New Year's Day,
a day of moving ahead,
of leaving behind,
of standing before
the future.
        —THOMAS L. REID

May your joys be many
and the tears be few;
peace to the world
and much love to you.
—PATTY FORBES CHENG

We pray we may sift
wrong from right,
strength from weakness,
have courage, might,
to live with wholeness
all of our days,
to be loving and kind,
as we give God praise.
        —NORMA WOODBRIDGE

Here's to the blessings of the year,
Here's to the friends we hold so dear,
To peace on earth, both far and near!

NEW YEAR'S RESOLUTION

Look back fondly, look ahead bravely.
Hold dearly to what matters, let go of what doesn't.
Share a smile, shed a tear.
Give generously, receive graciously, love unconditionally.
Forgive when you can't.
Reach out, reach up,
Care.

—SANDRA E. MCBRIDE

For auld lang syne, my dear,
for auld lang syne.
We'll take a cup of kindness yet
for auld lang syne.

—ROBERT BURNS

VALENTINE'S DAY

May our love always be as courageous
and forgiving as a child taking its first steps.
May our love open wide like the petals
of the magnolia revealing its perfect imperfection.
May our love be as wild as the dance
of fireflies, as joyful as Handel's
Hallelujah Chorus, as playful as river otters,
as satisfying as a bowl of soup on a cold day.
Yes, all these things and more, more, more.
　　—SUSAN J. ERICKSON

VALENTINE
· · · · · · · · ·

At this moment
and always
you are holding
my heart in your hands.
—CORRINE DE WINTER

Outside, the snow
is wintry bright.
Inside, my heart's
a warm delight.
Be my Valentine.
    —PATRICIA CRANDALL

ST. PATRICK'S DAY

May your neighbors respect you,
Trouble neglect you,
The angels protect you,
And heaven accept you.

May the Irish hills caress you.
May her lakes and rivers bless you.
May the luck of the Irish enfold you.
May the blessings of Saint Patrick behold you.

May your blessings outnumber
The shamrock that grow,
And may trouble avoid you
Wherever you go.

APRIL FOOLS' DAY

TO FOOLISH FUN!

Friends, you can fool me once!
Friends, you can fool me twice!
Here's to lots of foolish fun,
before this crazy day is done.
—BARBARA YOUNGER

Fools we are,
fools we will remain.
For what would life be without our foolish dreams!
—JUDY ACKLEY BROWN

Foolishness can breed good things—
Let April Fools' Day be your reminder.
—JILL FRANCES DAVIS

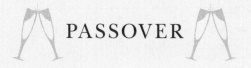

PASSOVER

LIBERATION

On Passover we speak liberation:
the freeing of the body to go its own way;
the freeing of the mind to think its own thoughts;
the freeing of the heart to feel its own fires;
the freeing of the soul to find its own place.

On Passover we speak of love:
the loving of the body and the coming to our senses;
the loving of the mind and the coming to sense;
the loving of the heart and the coming to Meeting;
the loving of the soul and the coming to Meaning.

May the spirit of Passover inspire us to liberate
our world for love.
Amen.

  —RABBI RAMI M. SHAPIRO

We were slaves,
now we are free.
To life, liberty, and freedom.
L'chayim!
—PAULA E. KIRMAN

PASSOVER TOAST
· · · · · · · · · · · ·

L'dor v'dor, from generation to generation,
we retell the story.

May tonight's retelling give us the courage
to follow in the footsteps of our people,
to step into the swirling sea,
to create the future we envision.
—MARCIA SZYMANSKI

Vehotzeiti, Vehitzalti, Vega'alti, Velakachti
(the four words of redemption)

EASTER

LET ALL CREATION SING!

More than bunnies, painted eggs
And pleasant toasts to Spring:
For souls reborn on Easter morn,
Let all creation sing!
—E. SHAN CORREA

May your dog find the last hidden Easter egg
before July 4th!
—JANET LOMBARD

May Easter leave our hearts
filled with resurrected hope.
May Easter leave our lives
filled with resurrected love.
—ANNE CALODICH FONE

To the stone rolled away
on this Easter day;
to Christ and his wounds,
risen up from the tomb.

—NANCY TUPPER LING

Khristós Anésti! Alithós Anésti!
Christ has risen; he has risen indeed!

—THE PASCHAL GREETING, USED IN MOST ORTHODOX CHURCHES

A blessing is Easter
joy in the morning
hope in tomorrow
peace inside.

—PAULA TIMPSON

MOTHER'S DAY

A mother's love is like a circle, it has no beginning and no ending. It keeps going around and around, ever expanding, touching everyone who comes in contact with it.

—ART URBAN

The most important thing she'd learned over the years was that there was no way to be a perfect mother, and a million ways to be a good one.

—JILL CHURCHILL

My mother had a great deal of trouble with me,
but I think she enjoyed it.

—MARK TWAIN

A MOTHER'S DAY GRACE

It's an impossible job.

No one can ever do it perfectly.

Be willing to accept that there is no success or failure here.

Let us give up the burden of unreal expectations.

Let us cherish what is and nourish each other's dreams.

Let us remember the best and forgive the rest.

Allow all the love that may have

slipped into tight places free now

to illuminate the harmony

that always existed

at the very center

of our hearts.

—ARLENE GAY LEVINE

A TOAST TO MOTHER

Mother, you were
always my biggest
fan when I succeeded,
my greatest comfort
when I failed.

    —THOMAS L. REID

BLESS ALL MOTHERS

Bless all mothers.
They loved us before knowing us.
They cherished us before
we had done anything memorable,
and yet they requested only
that we be born healthy and wail strong.
They saw our greatness from the start.
Bless all mothers.

    —ZORAIDA RIVERA MORALES

God could not be everywhere and therefore he made mothers.

    —JEWISH PROVERB

A MOTHER'S DAY BLESSING

Bless the mother whose child is sick, and bless the one whose child is well. Bless the mother who helps with homework, who cooks a meal, who sits on the floor to play, and who goes to her knees to pray. Bless the young mother with a child in her womb, and the old mother whose child is grown. And bless the mother whose child has a child of her own. Bless them all, as bound together, they bind us all.

—EVE LOMORO

DEAR MOM

You are
blessed, and such a blessing,
loved, and so loving,
a gift, and so giving,
a treasure, and so treasured!
For you, and to you,
I am forever grateful.

—SUSANNE WIGGINS BUNCH

She cooks the roast and washes dishes
Offers hugs and healing kisses
Does the laundry, drives the car
Chauffeurs kids both near and far
Cleans up messes, packs the lunch
Laughs a lot and smiles a bunch
Helps her children learn and grow
And when it's time, she lets them go.
—MICHELLE HEIDENRICH BARNES

To Mom,
God gave you the strength to hold me close
and the wisdom to let me go.
Here's to the gift of a mother—my mother!
—SANDRA E. MCBRIDE

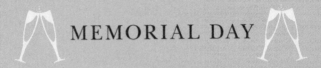

MEMORIAL DAY

REST IN GLORY

In honor of all those
who died that
we might live in peace;

may Heaven celebrate
their glory and honor
their lives.

—SALLY CLARK

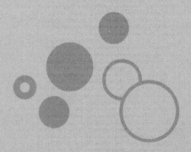

FOR MEMORIAL DAY

· · · · · · · · · · · · · · ·

(from the Gettysburg Address)

The world will little note, nor long remember,
what we say here, but it can never forget what they
did here. It is for us the living, rather, to be dedicated
here to the unfinished work which they who fought
here have thus far so nobly advanced. It is rather for
us to be here dedicated to the great task remaining
before us—that from these honored dead we take
increased devotion to that cause for which they
gave the last full measure of devotion—that we here
highly resolve that these dead shall not have died
in vain…

—ABRAHAM LINCOLN

Here's to our heroes
and loved ones lost,
who defended our country,
no matter the cost.
—JILL N. MACGREGOR

On this Memorial Day let us remember
those who fought and died that we may
live in a free land. May we conduct
ourselves in such a way that their sacrifice
may not be in vain.

—SALLY JADLOW

With selfless service of valor and deed,
defending our country in time of need,
at home, overseas or far away,
close in our prayers you'll always stay.

—JILL N. MACGREGOR

FATHER'S DAY

The words that a father speaks to his children in the privacy of home are not heard by the world, but, as in whispering galleries, they are clearly heard at the end, and by posterity.

—JEAN PAUL RICHTER

To Dad—
your words were gentle,
your actions humble,
your arms strong,
ready to hold
your weary child.

Now that I've grown,
I raise a glass
to toast everything
you were and are to me.

—NANCY TUPPER LING

To Dad,

may the love and respect we express toward you

make up for the worry and care we have visited upon you.

TO MY FATHER, A TOAST

If faith is the assurance of things hoped for,

the conviction of things not seen,

I have the courage to believe today

because I have seen you

live,

dream,

work,

play,

and love—

without limit.

—MARYANNE HANNAN

Providing love, guidance, and support,

fathers are heroes in disguise

and their example is destined

to transform and shape our lives.

—SHEILA WIPPERMAN

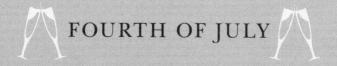

FOURTH OF JULY

Firework booms light the sky
we celebrate our nation's birth;
may stars and stripes forever bless
the greatest nation on the earth.
—SALLY CLARK

As we prepare to ooh and aah
over the artwork in the sky,
here's to fireworks,
here's to summer,
and here's to America
on this festive Fourth of July!
—BARBARA YOUNGER

Here's to everywhere we're from and everywhere we'll be,
To miracles that brought us together in this country.
—PEG DUTHIE

Here's to our nation—
May she always realize
that order alone can
not help the helpless,
that government without
compassion only separates
us from ourselves.
—THOMAS L. REID

On this day in 1776, the colonies declared their independence from
Great Britain.
Two hundred thirty-_____years and many generations ago.
Certainly long enough to justify this drink and several more.
To America!
—JANICE A. FARRINGER

May this day of flags and fireworks
ever remind us of our freedom
and spark in us new appreciation
for this, our Independence Day.
—CHARMAINE PAPPAS DONOVAN

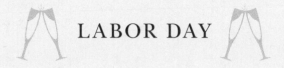

LABOR DAY

LABOR DAY! LET'S PARTY!

Welcome, hard workers,
be our guest,
let's party hard,
on this day of rest!

—BARBARA YOUNGER

On this Labor Day, we toast Francis Perkins: as Secretary of Labor during Franklin Roosevelt's administration, she worked for working women and men, providing them with Social Security, a minimum wage, and unemployment insurance. Please raise your glasses in gratitude to her—and to all American workers.

—MARTHA K. BAKER

Here's to well-paid work
and well-earned rest!
—PEG DUTHIE

We devise ways to shorten our working life by strategies so clever,
Only to find out when we retire that we're busier than ever!
—SHEILA WIPPERMAN

HALLOWEEN

A HALLOWEEN PARTY TOAST

Here's to the ghosts
of Halloween past,
and here's to us,
let's have a blast!

—BARBARA YOUNGER

TRICKS OR TREATS

On Halloween night, we light our lanterns,
watch them flicker in ghostly patterns.

To masqueraders who roam the streets,
spare your tricks and receive our treats.

—SALLY CLARK

HAPPY HALLOWEEN

. . . .

To all the happy pumpkin faces
lighting up so many places.
Orange faces burning bright
in the cool October night.
—CHARLES GHIGNA

To witches, goblins, ghouls and ghosts,
I hereby offer up a toast.
—BARB MAYER

Halloween—the only time
you can act like a witch
and get rewarded with candy.
—SHEILA FORSYTH

DRINK, MY DEARS—IT'S HALLOWEEN!

Toasting you with eye of newt,
slug juice in a champagne flute,
gray puree of lizard spleen:
drink, my dears—
IT'S HALLOWEEN!
    —E. SHAN CORREA

THANKSGIVING

THANKSGIVING TOAST

Here's to giving thanks by filling our days
with acts of kindness and compassion.
There's no better way to show our gratitude than by living it.

—VICTORIA KENNEDY

For faith, for family, and friends,
for countless blessings that You send,
for food and shelter, health and love,
We give thanks to God above.

—SUSANNE WIGGINS BUNCH

A PRAYER OF THANKSGIVING

For leaves of yellow and scarlet,
for goldenrod's bright array,
for crisp November breezes,
and frisky squirrels at play;
for misted mornings and velvet nights,
for glowing harvest moon,
for crickets' tuneful chirping
on a sunny afternoon;
for families gathered together,
for marigolds in a bouquet,
for bounty from the earth to share
this blessed holiday,
we're thankful.
    —SHEILA FORSYTH

Grace is said across the land.
Each family makes a toast.
Of all who choose to give today,
Tom Turkey gives the most!
    —CHARLES GHIGNA

FOR THANKSGIVING

. . . .

(Soul Seeds)

The simplicity is overwhelming,
for what we plant, we also reap.

Lord, grant us soul seeds,
that we may plant them with love,
water them with tears of compassion,
nurture them with embraces of warmth,
protect them from the storms of life.

Bless this bounty with grace and gentleness,
that the harvest will be abundant
in love, in trust, to be shared
with those closest to our hearts.

May we plant soul seeds for strength,
harvested in hope this Thanksgiving,
for all the days and years that follow.

—JUDITH A. LINDBERG

We open wide the door to all
to spread some grateful cheer;
Thanksgiving is a time for friends
for those whom we hold dear.

—SYLVIA FORBES

Thanks and giving—
words for living
life with gratitude.
God, we pray—
endow this day
with sweet beatitude.

—E. SHAN CORREA

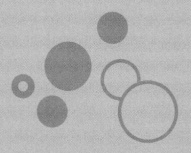

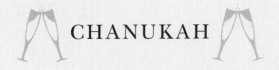

CHANUKAH

EACH CHANUKAH CANDLE

As we light each Chanukah candle,
And watch our children's faces,
We pray for understanding
Among people of all races.

—JILL WILLIAMS

Here's to our celebration,
our festival of lights;
menorahs, dreidels, latkes,
eight holiday days and nights.

—CHARLES GHIGNA

May this Chanukah be one of joyful embrace.
May we stand with the Macabees and affirm ourselves,
our people and our light,
and thus challenge the darkness of ignorance
with the light of meaning, hope, purpose, and love.

    —RABBI RAMI M. SHAPIRO

The candles burn;
the dreidels spin.
Let's raise a glass
to miracles, to light, to life:
L'Chayim!
—PAULA E. KIRMAN

CHANUKAH WISH

This is my Chanukah wish—
to kindle holy lights
so that at nightfall
the world is lit
with hope and wisdom
to fight against hatred, greed, and despair.
May the light be spread among the nations
and be like the twinkling of stars shining,
illuminating a path of love, goodness, and generosity.
  —SHERRI WAAS SHUNFENTHAL

CHRISTMAS

What can I give Him, poor as I am?
If I were a shepherd, I would bring a lamb;
if I were a wise man, I would do my part;
yet what can I give Him—give my heart.

—CHRISTINA ROSSETTI

A CHRISTMAS TOAST

To the holly and the ivy,
To the Christmas scent so sweet,
To all those who have gathered here,
You've made this day a treat!
—MARY MAUDE DANIELS

A CHRISTMAS GRACE

We thank Thee, dearest blessed Lord,
For all you've given us to share.
Come, fill our hearts with Christmas love
Your peace be here and everywhere.
Amen.

—FATHER PAUL KEENAN

Christmas…
a day when cheer and gladness blend,
when heart meets heart
and friend meets friend.

—J. H. FAIRWEATHER

A TOAST BEFORE OPENING THE PRESENTS

The best present
Of all this holiday
Is the presence
Of all of you!

—BARBARA YOUNGER

As we gather this Christmas Eve,
candles warm and welcoming before us,
the lights outside shining
bright in the darkness.
In the twinkle of the stars,
in the sparkle of the snow
lives Hope and Peace, Joy and Love.
For tonight was born in Bethlehem,
a baby boy, a Savior, a King.
To each of us is given in Him,
new life, new dreams, new promises,
new confidence in God,
a lifetime of goodness and mercy.
God Bless us, tonight and always.
To Hope, Peace, Joy, and Love.
Merry Christmas!
        —SYLVIA MASI

A TOAST TO CHRISTMAS PAST

Let's tip a glass to Christmas Past
and times we held so dear,
for now's the time to reminisce
and sip a bit of cheer.
Dwell not on sorrow in our lives
but raise our spirits high;
though cherished ones may go their way,
their memories never die.

Give prayer for virtues that we have,
forgive the ones we lack,
keep our sight on future goals
and failure at our back.
Make a vow to treasured friends
to always keep in touch—
the things we take for granted
are the ones that mean so much.

Live our lives as best we can
that peers may one day say:
we left the world a better place
because we passed this way.

    —C. DAVID HAY

This Christmas season,
may we be
joyful…
grateful…
wakeful…
to all the gifts we give
and receive.

—CHERYL PAULSON

CHRISTMAS JOY

Caroling voices, lovely voices,
singing songs of lowly birth,
fill our hearts with wondrous music.
Praise to God! Peace on earth!

—THOMAS L. REID

AN IRISH CHRISTMAS TOAST

May peace and plenty be the first
to lift the latch on your door,
and happiness be guided
to your home
by the candle of Christmas.

CHRISTMAS PRAYER

May the joy of the angels
that holy night
resound in your heart
and bring you delight.

May the faith of the shepherds
kneeling in prayer
remind you of God's love
everywhere.

May the wise men's devotion
that brought them so far
be also, for you,
a guiding star.

—THERESA MARY GRASS

THIS CHRISTMAS

May we set an extra place at the table this Christmas,
as we remember the hungry, the poor.
May we wrap an extra gift this Christmas, as we
remember the lonely, the confused.
May we give an extra hug this Christmas, as an
expression of love to those around us.
May we spend extra time in meditation this Christmas,
as we remember all the blessings we've received—
beautiful gifts of life and grace.

—NORMA WOODBRIDGE

A TOAST TO FAMILY AT CHRISTMAS

Outside snowflakes are falling.
There's winter in the air,
but in our house it's cozy
all because we are here.
Let's have a Merry Christmas
and the most wonderful New Year,
as we continue on through life,
with the family we hold dear.

—NOREEN BRAMAN

SHARE JOY!

May the star that shone in Bethlehem
brighten our path each day.

May Christ's light of peace and love
direct us on our way.

And may the joy the angels knew
be shared by us in all we do.

—THERESA MARY GRASS

A CHRISTMAS WISH

I wish you the joy of Christmas,
    the Season's sweet repose.
I wish you the peace of Christmas
    to mark the old year's close.
I wish you the hope of Christmas
    to cheer you on your way.
And a heart of faith and gladness
    to greet each coming day.

THE JOY OF GIVING

Somehow, not only for Christmas
but all the long year through,
the joy that you give to others
is the joy that comes back to you;
and the more you spend in blessing
the poor and lonely and sad:
the more of your heart's possessing
returns to make you glad.
—JOHN GREENLEAF WHITTIER

CHRISTMAS EVE BLESSING

May the mystical peace
of this blessed Christmas Eve
remain in our hearts
throughout the New Year.
—NOREEN BRAMAN

CHRISTMAS BENEDICTION

May your barns be full of plenty,
and your heart be full of song.
May your house be full of laughter,
and friends, the whole year long.

May your days be full of wonder,
merriment and peace,
with love and hope surrounding,
may Christmas joys increase.
—NORMA WOODBRIDGE

TINY TIM'S TOAST

(from *A Christmas Carol*)

Here's to us all!
God bless us every one!
—CHARLES DICKENS

KWANZAA

AFRICAN RHAPSODY

I give thanks to the Creator for all the blessings of this earth. I ask that the Spirit of Kwanzaa be infused into every aspect of my daily life. May the light of the seven candles illuminate my daily affairs and guide me into the fulfillment of my true potential. May I always remember my Ancestors with reverence and love. May I benefit from their wisdom and strength as I seek to preserve and continue the heritage they left me.

—X-RAY ROBINSON

Kinara candles burning bright,
our week of celebrations
full of feasts and festivals
and lots of cool libations.

—CHARLES GHIGNA

THE MEANING OF THE SEASON

Whether you light a Menorah,
trim a Christmas tree,
attend Midnight Mass,
or gather to share good food
and the lights of Kwanzaa

May you touch someone's heart,
give them hope,
put a smile on their face,
and share the meaning
of this special season.

—MARY MAUDE DANIELS

Author Index

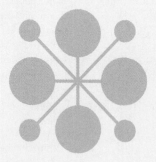

Permissions and Acknowledgments

Grateful acknowledgment is made to the authors and publishers for the use of the following material. Every effort has been made to contact original sources. If notified, the publishers will be pleased to rectify an omission in future editions.

Note: For any selection that appears without an attribution, we have determined through extensive research that the piece is "author unknown."

Elizabeth Adam for "A Dedication Prayer."
Caroline Joy Adams for "Peace in Our Homes."
  www.carolinejoyadams.com
Martha K. Baker for "On This Labor Day" and "We've Come Together to Remember."
Judy Barnes for "A Toast to Our Furry Companions."

Michelle Heidenrich Barnes for "Love Is Giving of Yourself" and "She Cooks the Roast." www.michellehbarnes.com

Carole Blake for "Here's to Everyone." www.cbpoems.com

Noreen Braman for "Christmas Eve Blessing" and "A Toast to Family at Christmas."

Danielle Brigante for "A Blessing for Family."

Judy Ackley Brown for "Blessing at a Pet Burial," "A Blessing for a Charity Event," "Dear God, Forgive Me," "Fools We Are," and "A Toast to Our Guests."

Susanne Wiggins Bunch for "Celebration Prayer," "Dear Mom," "For Faith, For Family, and Friends," and "A Toast to Our Abilities."

Elizabeth Campbell for "From This Day Forth."

Janine Canan for "Art Is Simply a Gift," "Artists Are the Rememberers," "I Followed the River," "Let Every Moment," and "Take This Life." www.janinecanan.com

Anya Cara for "Grace for a Gathering."

Kirsten Casey for "When I Think Back."

Patty Forbes Cheng for "May Your Joys Be Many."

Sally Clark for "At Your Table," "Because You Were Born," "Beginnings," "The Body Is Gone," "Congratulations on Your Achievements," "Families Remember," "A Family Is the Soil," "Firework Booms," "Here's to the Bride," "Milestone," "A Newlywed's Toast," "Now a Husband," "Rest in Glory," "The Taste of Success," "Then and Now," "To All That We May Accomplish," "To Our Flag," "To Your Success," and "Tricks or Treats." www.sallyclark.info

Deborah Gordon Cooper for "Heal Us" and "Memorial Prayer." www.cooperartpoetry.com

E. Shan Correa for "As You Depart," "Drink, My Dears—It's Halloween," "For This Food," "Let All Creation Sing!," and "Thanks and Giving."

June Cotner for "May Gratitude at Night." www.junecotner.com

Patricia Crandall for "Outside, the Snow."

Jim Croegaert for "On This Day's Road" and "To Friendship." www.roughstonesmusic.com

Mary Maude Daniels for "A Christmas Toast," "Gratitude," "Heart to Heart," "A House Blessing," "A Housewarming Toast," "The Meaning of the Season," "To the Artist Who Sees," and "Your World Is Vast."

Jill Frances Davis for "Foolishness Can Breed Good Things."

Corrine De Winter for "Valentine." www.corrinedewinter.com

Charmaine Pappas Donovan for "May This Day of Flags" and "To All the Milestones." www.charmainedonovan.com

Annie Dougherty for "Birthday Blessing," "Friendship Grace," "In the Name of All," "Morning, God," "The Time Is Gone," "To Reach," and "What a Joy to Join Together."

Sean Thomas Dougherty for "May You Climb Mountains."

Jan Dunlap for "A Marriage for All Seasons." www.jandunlap.com

Peg Duthie for "Here's to Everywhere We're From" and "Here's to Well-Paid Work." www.nashpanache.com

Lori Eberhardy for "The Answer."

Susan J. Erickson for "May Our Love Always Be."

Janice A. Farringer for "On This Day in 1776" and "Tonight We Dine." www.amidlifebooksandpoetry.com

Anne Calodich Fone for "May Easter," "May the Family Ties That Bind Us" and "To Health."

Sylvia Forbes for "May Your Feet Never Ache" and "We Open Wide the Door to All." www.heartlandwriter.com

Sheila Forsyth for "Halloween," "Praise for the New Year," and "A Prayer of Thanksgiving."

Donna Austgen Frisinger for "Let the Children Flourish." www.donnafrisinger.com

Diane M. Geiser for "Bless Our Soil," "May You Be Blessed By Your Dreams," and "They Age Us."

Charles Ghigna for "Art Is Undefinable," "Grace Is Said Across the Land," "Happy Halloween," "Here's to Creativity," "Here's to Our Celebration," "Kinara Candles Burning Bright," "May You Paint the Sunset," "Puppy Love," "A Toast to Autumn," "A Toast to Spring," "A Toast to Summer," "A Toast to Winter," and "You are My Star." www.fathergoose.com

Marilyn Huntman Giese for "Ship to Shore."

Michael S. Glaser for "A Blessing for Our Children," "A Christening Blessing," and "A Toast for New Beginnings." www.michaelsglaser.com

Benita Glickman for "Raise Your Glass."

Theresa Mary Grass for "Bless What We Eat," "Christmas Prayer," "Our Wish for You," "Share Joy!" and "Wherever You Go."

Annette Gulati for "Here's to a Future," "One Small Step," and "A Toast to the Graduate." www.annettegulati.com

Maryanne Hannan for "To My Father, a Toast." www.mhannan.com

Charlene Hasha for "Life Is Like a Roller Coaster."

C. David Hay for "A Toast to Christmas Past."

Melissa Hed for "Here's to Our Clients," "May Our Hunger Be Sated," "My Dear," and "To Our Success."

Barbara J. Holt for "In Celebration of a Newborn."

Gary W. Huffman for "In Celebration of the Family" and "Second Marriage" by Margaret Anne Huffman, excerpted from *Family Celebrations*, edited by June Cotner. Copyright © 1999. Published by Andrews McMeel Publishing.

Sally Jadlow for "On This Memorial Day." www.sallyjadlow.com

Victoria Kennedy for "Thanksgiving Toast."

Paula E. Kirman for "The Candles Burn," "In Your New Position" and "We Were Slaves." www.mynameispaula.com

Stephen Kopel for "A Grace for Friends."

Arlene Gay Levine for "May the Light," "A Mother's Day Grace," "One," and "You Were Always in Our Hearts." www.arlenegaylevine.com

Judith A. Lindberg for "Counting Blessings" and "For Thanksgiving."

Nancy Tupper Ling for "Home Never Leaves Your Heart," "If I Could Search," "To Dad," "To the Stone Rolled Away," and "A Weeping Willow Prayer." www.nancytupperling.com

Janet Lombard for "The Gift of Your Friendship" and "May Your Dog."

Eve Lomoro for "A Mother's Day Blessing." www.evelomoro.blogspot.com

Barbara Boothe Loyd for "May Your Days Be Many."

Jill N. MacGregor for "Here's to Our Heroes," "Isn't It Good," "May Good Things and Blessings," "May This, Your Day," "Our Hearts Are Full," "With Selfless Service," "You've Earned Your Degree," and "You've Put in Your Time."

Andrea L. Mack for "Today Is Yours," excerpted from *House Blessings*, edited by June Cotner. Copyright © 2004. Published by Cotner Ink. Distributed by Chronicle Books. www.andrea-mack.blogspot.com

Sylvia Masi for "As We Gather This Christmas Eve."

Barb Mayer for "From the Joy of Discovery," "Here's to Fortune," "It Is Said," "Retirement Means," "To Adventures," "To the Act of Giving," and "To Witches, Goblins, Ghouls and Ghosts." www.barbmayer.com

Sandra E. McBride for "Be You," "New Year's Resolution," and "To Mom."

Eric Kobb Miller for "Here's to Change," "Here's to Having Plans B through Z," "Here's to Our Food," "Here's to Our Humor," "Here's to *Que Sera Sera*," and "Here's to Singing the Song in Our Heart." www.spittoonssaloon.blogspot.com

Michelle Close Mills for "Like Rings of a Tree." www.authorsden.com/michelleclosemills

Reverend Phyllis Ann Min for "A Wedding Blessing." www.phylliswithjoy.com

Barbara J. Mitchell for "May You Live."

Carol Murray for "A Child's Grace" and "Here's to Years of Happiness."

Leslie A. Neilson for "The Gift" and "On Your Wedding Day."

Joan Noëldechen for "A Toast to Your Life's Journey."

Beatrice O'Brien for "May All Your Campsites."

Karen O'Leary for "Success Sparkles." www.whispersinthewind333.blogspot.com

Marian Olson for "Every End Is a Beginning."

Carl "Papa" Palmer for "I Celebrate This Day." www.authorsden.com/carlpalmer

Paul A. Keenan Memorial Foundation for "A Christmas Grace" by Father Paul Keenan, excerpted from *Christmas Blessings*, edited by June Cotner. Copyright © 2002. Published by Warner Books. www.fatherpaul.com

Cheryl Paulson for "This Christmas Season."
www.breathingroomcenter.com

Susan Paurazas for "Thank You for This Yummy Food."

James Penha for "Despite Months and Miles Away."
www.jamespenha.com

Mary Lenore Quigley for "At Our Meeting's End," "I Love God," "May You Prosper Every Day," "No Matter How Long Ago," "To Everyone Here Today," and "To Fortitude and Perseverance." www.q2ink.com

Licia Rando for "A Grace of Care" and "A Toast to Old Dogs."
www.liciarando.com

DeMar Regier for "Here's to Flinging That Mortarboard Cap" and "I'm Thankful."

Thomas L. Reid for "Christmas Joy," "Eternal Creator," "Here's to Having Fun," "Here's to Our Nation," "May We Know," "May We Realize," "A Toast to Mother," "A Wedding Toast," and "We Toast New Year's Day."

Zoraida Rivera Morales for "Bless All Mothers," "Listen," and "Retirement."

Linda Robertson for "I Decided a Long Time Ago."

Jo-Anne Rowley for "Bless the Children."

John Runyard for "To My Children" by Gwen Tremain Runyard, excerpted from *House Blessings*, edited by June Cotner. Copyright © 2004. Published by Cotner Ink. Distributed by Chronicle Books. www.runyard.org

Sara Sanderson for "As the Heavens Play" and "May Comets Streaking Overhead."

Wendy L. Schmidt for "Don't Waste Your Time." shesgotashortfuse.blogspot.com and bumpynightpublications.blogspot.com

Doris Schuchard for "Light a Candle."

Joanne Seltzer for "Enjoy."

Rabbi Rami M. Shapiro for "Liberation" and "May This Chanukah." www.rabbirami.com

Sheri Waas Shunfenthal for "Be Daring," "Chanukah Wish," and "Now Is the Time."

Joel A. Singer for three selections by James Broughton: "Happiness Takes a Risk," "Hooray for the Inevitable," and "Thanks to the Sun." "Happiness Takes a Risk" was posted on http://bigjoyproject.tumblr.com/post/48544324106/happiness-takes-a-risk-misery-plays-it-safe. "Hooray for the Inevitable" by James Broughton was excerpted from his poem, "The Last Sermon of Gnarley Never," published in *Special Deliveries: New and Selected Poems*, edited by Mark Thompson. Copyright © 1990 by James Broughton. Published by Broken Moon Press, PO Box 24585, Seattle, WA 98124. "Thanks to the Sun" by James Broughton was published in *Amazing Graces*, edited by June Cotner. Copyright © 2001 by June Cotner. Published by HarperCollins. Used with permission from Joel A. Singer www.joelasinger.com

Anne Spring for "Family Re-Union" and "This Present Day."

Joan Stephen for "Philosophy."

Norman Styers for "To Our Friends Who Made School Fun."

Ramnath Subramanian for "The World Is Jeweled."

Marcia Szymanski for "Passover Toast." www.marciaszymanski.com

Nancy Tandon for "May the Path of Life Lead You."
www.nancytandon.com

Paula Timpson for "Art Is the Imagination," "A Blessing Is Easter," "A Toast to Marriage," and "What Gifts Children Are." www.paulaspoetryworld.blogspot.com

Ruth Treeson for "Here's to Creativity and Imagination."

Donna Wahlert for "To Our Guests," "Today We Gather," and "We Send You On Your Journey."

Louise I. Webster for "Old Glory," "Raise a Glass to Fighting Dragons," and "To the Joining of Hands."

Sheila Wipperman for "Here's to the Definition," "Learn from the Past," "Providing Love," and "We Devise Ways."

Norma Woodbridge for "Christmas Benediction," "This Christmas," "Toast to the New Year," and "We Pray."

Donna Wyland for "Enjoy Your Reward," "Great Visions," "Have Fun," and "We Honor You." www.donnawyland.com

Barbara Younger for "As We Prepare to Ooh and Aah," "As You Venture Forth," "At the Grave of a Fine Cat," "Birthday Grace," "A Blessing for a Hike," "A Halloween Party Toast," "A Hot Chocolate Toast," "Labor Day! Let's Party!," "My Place, a Table Grace," "To Art!," "To Foolish Fun!" "A Toast Before Opening the Presents," "A Toast to the Tooth Fairy," and "Welcome, New Kitten." www.friendfortheride.com

Kathryn Schultz Zerler for "Prayer in Three Simple Steps."

About the Coauthors

JUNE COTNER is the author or editor of thirty books, including the bestselling *Graces, Bedside Prayers,* and *House Blessings.* Her books altogether have sold nearly one million copies and have been featured in many national publications, including *USA Today, Better Homes & Gardens, Woman's Day,* and *Family Circle.* June has appeared on national television and radio programs.

June's latest love and avocation is giving presentations on "Adopting Prisoner-Trained Shelter Dogs." In 2011, she adopted Indy, a chocolate lab/Doberman mix (a LabraDobie!), from the Freedom Tails program at Stafford Creek Corrections Center in Aberdeen, Washington. June works with Indy daily to build on the wonderful obedience skills he mastered in the program. She and Indy have appeared on the television shows *AM Northwest* (Portland, OR) and *New Day Northwest* (Seattle).

A graduate of the University of California at Berkeley, June is the mother of two grown children and lives in Poulsbo, Washington with her husband. Her hobbies include yoga, hiking, and playing with her two grandchildren.

For more information, please visit June's website at www.junecotner.com.

 NANCY TUPPER LING is a children's author, poet, and librarian. She has great fun teaching poetry to grade school children, high school students, fellow poets, and senior citizens. She is the author of *Laughter in My Tent; My Sister, Alicia May; Character;* and *Coming Unfrozen*. She is the author of the forthcoming children's book, *Double Happiness*, which will be published by Chronicle Books in Fall 2015.

Nancy was the winner of the *Writer's Digest* Grand Prize for her poem "White Birch." Chosen from over 18,000 selections, this was the first time a poem won over all other categories including screenplays, poetry, fiction, nonfiction, short story, children's and YA.

In 2002, she founded the Fine Line Poets. She has served as poetry judge and library liaison for the Massachusetts State Poetry Society.

For more information, visit her websites at www.nancytupperling.com and www.finelinepoets.com.

TO OUR READERS

Viva Editions publishes books that inform, enlighten, and entertain. We do our best to bring you, the reader, quality books that celebrate life, inspire the mind, revive the spirit, and enhance lives all around. Our authors are practical visionaries: people who offer deep wisdom in a hopeful and helpful manner. Viva was launched with an attitude of growth and we want to spread our joy and offer our support and advice where we can to help you live the Viva way: vivaciously!

We're grateful for all our readers and want to keep bringing you books for inspired living. We invite you to write to us with your comments and suggestions, and what you'd like to see more of. You can also sign up for our online newsletter to learn about new titles, author events, and special offers.

Viva Editions
2246 Sixth St.
Berkeley, CA 94710
www.vivaeditions.com
(800) 780-2279
Follow us on Twitter @vivaeditions
Friend/fan us on Facebook